Praise for

girl·Logic

"Iliza is funny, fierce, and lightning fast…Take my advice: Take her advice. Iliza is a comedian wrapped in social critic wrapped in the good friend you need."

—Robbie Myers, former editor-in-chief of *ELLE* magazine

"Iliza Shlesinger's brand of feminist comedy is quick, smart, and doesn't suffer fools.…A gifted stand-up comic, Shlesinger…is a nuanced feminist and a comic with the instincts and sensibility to address women's rights while inviting men—who in her humor can be monosyllabic and imposing but is mostly well-meaning if misguided—inside the tent.… [*Girl Logic*] is a call for women to celebrate themselves and not succumb to fashion, politics, and media that often degrade them."

—*Los Angeles Times*

"*Girl Logic* delves into the complicated inner monologue it takes to be a female on this planet.… [It] reads as a more introspective and personal version of her 2016 Netflix special *Confirmed Kills*, which I show to anyone I think is in need of a deep belly laugh."

—*Washington Post*'s *The Lily*

"Softly polemic and brutally hilarious, *Girl Logic* is for women with a sense of humor, and women who aren't afraid to use it."

—Powells.com

"[Shlesinger] expertly explores the 'secret genius of irrational behavior' in this irreverent and insightful collection."

—*InTouch* magazine

"The takeaway messages of the book are important: cultivate confidence, develop the courage to be different, refuse catty competition with other women." —*Kirkus Reviews*

"Iliza not only has a way with words, she also has an observational intensity that pushes those words into your brain with comedic fury."

—Marc Maron, comedian, actor, author, and host of the popular podcast *WTF with Marc Maron*

"Hilarious." —*Star* magazine

"Shlesinger built her comedic voice around discussing how women think, and her book explores girl logic's rationale in impressive detail." —Refinery29.com

"Iliza Shlesinger [is] one of my favorite comedians....*Girl Logic* [is] Iliza's take on why women do what they do....It's a really interesting time to have a book about the way women think and see the world when we're having these big conversations about men."

—Sam Sanders, NPR's *It's Been a Minute with Sam Sanders*

"The book is full of wisdom and humor and the kind of confessions that make you feel like you *know* a celebrity, even when all you've done is read something they wrote.... But the best part is that she gives advice—real, honest advice about how to navigate the world as a strong woman who questions everything and kowtows to no one."
—*Glam*

"Iliza is a fearless comedian because she is a fearless woman.... She sees deeply, she thinks deeply, and she feels deeply.... [F]ind yourself in the pages of this book. Your hurt, your fear, and your loneliness will be remedied time and again with the laughter and the wisdom of a woman who will teach you to fight for your self-identification as a warrior and your destiny as a woman."
—Mayim Bialik, star of CBS's *The Big Bang Theory* and *NYT* bestselling author of *Girl Up!*

"One of my all-time favorite books...I already feel like I need to re-read to fully appreciate and I know it's one I can return to throughout my life."
—*The Unfinished Bookshelf*

"*Girl Logic* is a hilarious approach to friendship, singlehood, and relationships."
—TheSocial.ca

"I loved Iliza's book! It had me laughing at many points throughout. But it also had me thinking about the way I treat others and how I treat myself. I recommend this book to anyone."
—*Some Shenanagins*

(g)irl·Logic

{ *the genius and the absurdity* }

ILIZA
SHLESINGER

hachette
BOOKS
NEW YORK   BOSTON

Hachette Books
Hachette Book Group
1290 Avenue of the Americas, New York, NY 10104
hachettebooks.com
twitter.com/hachettebooks

Originally published in hardcover and ebook by Perseus Books in
November 2017
First trade paperback edition: October 2018

Hachette Books is a division of Hachette Book Group, Inc.
The Hachette Books name and logo are trademarks of Hachette Book Group, Inc.

The publisher is not responsible for websites (or their content)
that are not owned by the publisher.

The Hachette Speakers Bureau provides a wide range of authors for speaking events.
To find out more, go to www.hachettespeakersbureau.com or call (866) 376-6591.

Print book interior design by Cindy Young

ISBN: 978-1-6028-6334-7

Printed in the United States of America

LSC-C

10 9 8 7 6 5 4

For the girls.

Contents

Foreword

Mayim Bialik

It's hard to know where to begin when you talk about Iliza Shlesinger. It's hard to describe her. It's harder still to be the woman writing a foreword in a book written by Iliza Shlesinger.

Let's start with what we see on the outside. As a character actress who has struggled with my appearance and others' judgments about my appearance since I was nine years old, I know that Iliza is a stunner. It doesn't take but a glance to see it: her eyes, her cheekbones, her skin, her lips, and that sweet nose—she is pretty and cute and gorgeous all at once. Her body is fiercely strong and sexy, and her clothing choices on and off stage convey a confidence and an eccentricity that is enviable. She isn't afraid to be called hot, because she totally is.

But the outside of Iliza is not the only way I think or talk about her; and it's no longer even one of the first things I think about. Iliza is a comedian, a philosopher, a performer, and a business force to be reckoned with. She is a girl with logic that defies logic, and she is a woman who breaks rules I didn't even know existed. Iliza is devoted and loving and kind and she is generous and tender and protective. That's who she is and that's what she brings to life.

What struck me most about Iliza when I first found her on a weepy lonely night in my living room—I had recently had a break up from a significantly fantastic man I was still in love with—was that she was smart as a whip. She possesses a wisdom and a self-reflection that is rarely seen in any comedian; and I certainly was not used to a female comedian speaking the way she does and breaking the universe down the way she does.

Iliza is a fearless comedian because she is a fearless woman. Her brain does not work the way your brain or mine works—and you can trust me on this: I'm a doctor. Iliza's brain doesn't just see a "thing": she sees all the things that made the thing the thing and she simultaneously sees all the reasons the thing should be something else but isn't and she simultaneously sees the ways the thing could be better and she manages to communicate incredibly clearly and directly everything you need to know—and some things you may not need to know—about that thing. She sees deeply, she thinks deeply, and she feels deeply. She leaves no stone unturned. Ever.

It would be enough in the world of comedy if Iliza Shlesinger simply did what she does so well once; if she told one joke or one story with her wisdom and her insight and her skill, it would be *dayenu*, as we Jews say—it would be enough. If she did this in one set, in one bar, in one Netflix special, it would be *dayenu*.

But that's not how she does it. Iliza does this night after night, week after week, month after month and year after year. She does it in more than one Netflix special, and she brings herself to late night, and she has brought you the book you are now holding in your hand.

Girl Logic feels like a book by a comedian plenty of times. There are gems from her funny brain that had me laughing out loud again and again. But *Girl Logic* is also a guide for girls and women. Because Iliza doesn't live to make you laugh; she lives and writes to make you think. And consider. And weigh your options. Heels versus flats or fake tits (her words!) versus real, speak up or stay silent are decisions many women will encounter in their lives. She knows this, and she has lived inside of her brilliant brain for a long time while observing the lives of girls and women. She knows better than us in most cases, I promise.

Girl Logic surprised me most because it also feels like a memoir. But not in the sappy annoying way. And Iliza is the first to tell us she doesn't want to write a memoir. Her childhood was not tragic—it was not without its complexity, but she makes it clear that she is not an angry comic whose life led her to a world of laughter so that she wouldn't cry. What Iliza has done is to draw strength from her challenges and come out on top of every obstacle intellectually, spiritually, and emotionally.

Girl Logic opens up a part of Iliza's brain that I didn't know she was ready to share: it's the part that has been hurt. It's the part that is sometimes afraid. It's the part that wants very badly to be loved and sometimes doesn't know how. And it's the part that proves what a warrior she is in an industry which can take your sword, your shield, and your faith daily.

Iliza Shlesinger is someone you may not always agree with. You may not always like her. And you may not always want to hear what she has to say, but God help you if you can't find yourself in the pages of this book. Your hurt, your fear, and your loneliness will be remedied time and again with the laughter and the wisdom of a woman who will teach you to fight for your self-identification as a warrior, and your destiny as a woman.

Girl Logic

It Doesn't Mean You're "Crazy"—
It Just Means You're a Girl

Women aren't crazy. We are not crazy. We are conflicted. Crazy implies an impracticality to our thoughts when, in actuality, we are processing so many dichotomic thoughts that we get frustrated. Then others perceive that as "crazy." Women want to be appreciated for their mind, but they won't stop obsessing over the size of their ass. We tell you what we want, then get mad because you didn't realize that what we said isn't actually what we meant. We spend hours rehashing details or distinctions that men fail to notice, much less care about. ("I used a *peach gold* highlighter, not rose gold!") In any given day—hell, in the span of a few hours—we might want to be worshipped, sexualized, respected, dominated, held, or simply left alone. Depends on who's around, what we ate, temperature on Venus, all kinds of factors.

Are women crazy? Or stupid? No. (Well, don't get me wrong—*some* women are fucking crazy. And, OK, some are a little stupid—as are some men.) On the contrary, women are both afflicted and empowered by something I call Girl Logic. GL is a characteristically female way of thinking that *appears* to be contradictory and circuitous but is actually a complicated and highly evolved way of considering every choice and its repercussions before we make a move toward what we want.

What we want could be a great job, a hot dude, world domination, or a chicken sandwich—doesn't matter. Girl Logic kicks in and makes us ponder the past, present, and future all at the same time: "Well, maybe I could like this guy. But he's wearing a fedora and has a snaggletooth. But the last three good-looking guys I dated were horrible. But what if he'd be a great dad? But I'm not interested in having kids right now. I'm definitely not into him. But I might be later? OK, I'm giving him my number and texting him when I'm bored or drunk." All this internal back-and-forth might sound maddening, but what Girl Logic is truly doing is helping to prioritize our needs and values in both the short *and* long term. It's anything but crazy.

At its best, Girl Logic is a critical asset: an internal guidance system that helps women stay on track toward the thing—or person—they want most, or the woman they most want to be. It can admittedly also kick in at the weirdest moments as we try to sort out what we want right now versus what we want later. For instance, let's say some less-than-savory guy you've been trying to decide whether to go out with FINALLY texts you back after six hours of ignoring you. Let's say you put aside that six hours of silent rage you just experienced and you agree to go to the movies with him. Then . . . what about snacks? Girl Logic kicks in to help suss out your desires (Sour Patch Kids dumped in buttered popcorn, duh) and measure them against how you'll feel once that desire is met (like a pigeon who ate too much wedding rice). Then it weighs that outcome with how you feel that day (tired and bloated) against how you *want* to feel (like Gwyneth Paltrow* on a juice cleanse), against reality (you're gonna feel gross, so maybe just a few pieces? Or have all of it, but with bottled water, and promise to work out extra hard for the next three days but won't).

While I believe Girl Logic is ultimately designed to help us, it can sometimes feel like a curse. GL can go a little haywire when forced to reconcile the sheer volume of expectations society places on women. See, being a woman is hard. (And to that one guy who bought this to try to "expand his mind," don't you DARE set this book down now. Adjust your sack, hunker down, and at least read a few more pages before you go back to your fantasy draft.)

---

* FYI, I picked a white woman because it's harder for us to stay young looking. Also I have a better shot at looking like G.P. than I do of looking like Beyoncé.

Most of us don't even realize all the social pressures that weigh on us from the second we wash our faces in the morning to the moment we scrape off our sunscreen, primer, concealer, cover-up, bronzer, and blush every night. The truth is that women are supposed to be everything to everyone. And guess what?

That's impossible.

We're expected to be continually kind to our fellow women, caring toward children, respectful of the elderly, supportive of our coworkers—while simultaneously making every dude around us super horny. Oh and we should always stand up for ourselves, while also being likeable. DON'T FORGET TO BE LIKEABLE!

We're supposed to look eternally young while aging gracefully, and look hot while remaining "respectable." We're supposed to be open and vulnerable but without getting "too emotional," be sexually empowered but not "slutty." We're encouraged to eat whatever we want while our bodies are scrutinized for unruly curves, because men like a woman who eats, not a woman who *looks* like she eats.

Without even meaning to, we've internalized these social expectations and let them shape everything we do, say, feel, and believe. And then we spend way too much time trying to live up to unrealistic standards that were put in place before anyone reading this book was even born. Being expected to be perfect in every conceivable way—from the things we think, to the amount of makeup we wear, to the way we parent, run a business, have sex, or recover after childbirth—can be mind numbing and cause our GL to blow a fuse (or, worse, cause us to cry in public or cut our own hair).

One simple way to illustrate Girl Logic is with the common mealtime question, "What do you want to eat?" Most men will, perhaps unthinkingly, perhaps out of an attempt to accommodate, blurt out whatever sounds good and easy. To them, most things are black and white: "Pizza sounds cool" (probably because they won't have their worth be judged by how good they look in a fun top).

But women live in the gray, bathe in the gray, and summer in the gray. There are more than fifty shades of it, many of which don't involve S&M. We invariably consider the past, present, *and* future when making any choice because for us the stakes are higher emotionally (because we care about consequences) or just logistically (because we are aware of consequences in the first place). If you pick the wrong shoes, your feet could end up killing you all night . . . and tomorrow. If you push back against a coworker, you could lose your job or be harassed, ostracized, or labeled a bitch. If you text a guy after not hearing back, he might start referring to you as a desperate psycho. All these possibilities are constantly floating through our heads when considering any situation, including dinner. So instead of saying "pizza," we'll take into account what we're wearing at present (too tight for pizza?), what we might wear this evening, what we might be drinking, the potential messiness factor, and if the crust is made from wheat.

The pizza conundrum only highlights the ongoing battle between how we see ourselves, versus how we *want* to see

ourselves, versus how everyone else sees us. All of these con-
flicting directives are exhausting to process and can leave
women spinning in circles, headed in the wrong direction, or
simply crashing and burning. (And by crashing and burning
I mean that feeling where you're like, "I'm gonna be so healthy
this week," and at the end of Monday you're rationalizing, "If
I don't finish the whole pint *now,* I'll just have to eat more of
it tomorrow.")

It's no surprise that in so many woman-centered TV shows,
books, and movies, the main character suffers from a multiple
personality disorder: "a wife, mother, cop, alien . . . and trying
to balance it all!" When the heroine doesn't have kids, she's still
a mishmash of familiar stereotypes: "Chloe's trying to find Mr.
Right but is weird about commitment because she's been hurt
before! Can she carry an overflowing cup of coffee *and* maintain a high-powered career? Can she make it work? WILL
LOVE FIND HER?!" I mean, can you think of *any* lead male
character pitched as "ever-frazzled Scott is trying to balance
work, fathering, marriage, *and* his exhausting recreational ten-
nis team? Also, the poor thing is kind of a klutz!"

(Have you noticed that women are *always* klutzy when they
are supposed to be adorable? Falling into boxes, knocking over
food, walking while trying to look hot. Sandra Bullock, Anne
Hathaway, Drew Barrymore . . . apparently men like a klutz.
Not only because falling is funny but also I suspect because being clumsy makes you seem less powerful. Plus if they're falling
down they can't emasculate you!)

This book is both a commiseration and a celebration of Girl Logic. I'll discuss the way we collectively think but also give you some insight into my own personal experiences and how they connect to GL. I wrote it because I wanted to give women a break from the never-ending stream of nonsense in our mental in-box telling us we're wrong for feeling how we feel. "Psycho bitch," "bad feminist," "single weirdo," "mean girl," "crazy ex-girlfriend," "*female* comic"—these loaded labels are constantly applied to women as a way to write us off.

This book is my effort to help you tune out all that unnecessary chatter from within and without, and keep your GL working for you instead of against you. I wrote this book to let all girls know that whatever "psycho" thoughts you've had, I've had them, too. Sometimes my GL causes me to suffer a break with reality. I've been paralyzed between two outfits because one is sexy and one is comfortable, which leads to a fit of heavy scrutinizing (of both my clothes and my life choices).

I've censored myself in a conversation for fear of not being liked, only to replay it over and over, acting out different witty retorts should that exact conversation ever occur again. I've wolfed down a ham steak while thinking, "Whatever, I can just work out harder tomorrow." And then when tomorrow came and I was tired, I rationalized, "Whatever, I'll just eat less today." What a fun cycle of delusion!

And thanks to GL, nothing will send me into a mad rage more than texting a boy who doesn't write back. WE MADE OUT ONCE, AND I ASKED IF YOU WANTED TO GET

COFFEE—THIS DOESN'T HAVE TO BE COMPLICATED!
I SEE THE THREE DOTS MOVING, SCOTT, I KNOW
YOU'RE THERE!

But there is a method to the madness, as I'll show you in this book. See, GL can also work in positive ways. Yes GL will sometimes fill your head with exhausting thoughts and options. ("Do I really want to buy that, do that, eat that, date that?" A thousand reasons why "that" might not be a good idea to start from. . . .) But it can also be a rallying cry to take on the world. ("I've got this. I've totally got this. I've done it before, I can do it again, I will regret it forever if I don't DO IT RIGHT NOW!")

That's the great part of Girl Logic: it nudges us to push ourselves, question what we want, and refine our own ideas about what will make us happier, better people.

It's GL that keeps us engaged in sooooo many more things than men could even *dream* of doing. Just imagine your mom, or your aunt, or your best friend's mom. You know, all those real-life sixtysomething women taking a Spanish class on Monday night, a pottery class on Tuesday, attending a lecture on Wednesday, seeing the opera on Thursday, an art opening on Friday, and doing educational yoga retreats each summer. Sometimes their GL is working overtime trying to help them figure out what would make them happy: "I'm Sheryl! I'm taking an earthenware formation class while learning about mushroom whispering. I'm flirting with bead making, but cooking with sustainable thoughts is my new passion." (And just because you took on Oprah and Deepak's Twenty-One-Day Meditation Experience and only got through Day 3 doesn't mean you failed; it means you are three days closer to being the person you wanted to be . . . or *thought* you wanted to be.)

Now, think of your dad. He's probably had the same one or two hobbies all his life, right? OK, fine, maybe some dads eventually get into motorcycles or dating Asian women; my point exactly.

Understanding Girl Logic is a way of embracing both our aspirations and our contradictions. GL is the desire to be both strong and vulnerable. It's wanting to be curvy but rail thin at the same time. It's striving to kick ass in a man's world while still being loved by the women around you. Your GL is that little voice in your head that makes you aware of the practicality of your everyday choices, and how they'll shape your reality tomorrow: "If you don't read the *Washington Post* tonight, you will be left out of the conversation tomorrow." Of course there's always the dangling carrot of instant gratification: "But what I *really* need to do is unwind with some Instagram cake-decorating videos; I've earned it!" And . . . here comes GL again, swooping in to remind you how you felt last time you did that: "Didn't you say your New Year's resolution was being more informed?" It's your job to consider the options from every angle; your GL presents them all to you, and the one that weighs heaviest wins. "OK, I'll read a *Washington Post* tweet, THEN I can, unencumbered by guilt, watch these Snapchats of regional cheerleading competitions."

So why am I talking about this? Me, of all the people out there? No, I don't have a sociology degree, and I'm certainly not a psychologist. I'm a stand-up comic who has spent a

lifetime obsessed with questioning things and observing people—especially fellow women—and calling out the humor and
pathos in their/our contradictory behavior. I've collected a lot
of data, and now I get to put it in a book. I wanted to do a baking cookbook, but it would have been all blank pages; the last
page would just say, "I don't like chocolate, sorry."

This book is my attempt to continue that conversation, to
rip open my girl brain and spill it out for you, so you can say,
"Hey, wait—hers kinda looks like mine!" The truth is, *all*
women sometimes feel misunderstood, including me. I, too,
want thinner thighs. I, too, have freaked out at THAT BITCH
STACY after she got the promotion/gig/part I wanted. I, too,
have gotten pissed about not being pretty enough and then, in
the next breath, gotten even *more* pissed about the idea that I
have to look pretty at all.

But I love that I got to write this book for you. It's for all the
young girls who think they've figured it out (which is adorable,
but, because you're still shopping at LF, you . . . haven't). It's for
frustrated women in their twenties and thirties who *thought*
they had it all figured out until life was like, "WAIT 'TIL YOU
SEE MY DICK!" It's for older women, too, who might remi-
nisce about the good ol' confusing days as they give a throaty
laugh in their flowy Chico's pants.

And this book is also for *me* because apparently expound-
ing on stage for two hours a night wasn't enough. (Trust me, if
I could start a cult I would, but I hate the idea of deliberately
dying in a group.)

This book is a celebration of women in all our gray and all our glory. It's meant to remind you that no matter how kooky, conflicted, or off-kilter your Girl Logic may sometimes skew, that very same thinking bonds you with countless other women across the globe—and it serves a purpose. I promise.

1

You're a Woman—Be Confident!
("But Not So Confident That It Makes Anyone Else Insecure" Is Actually What They Mean)

I wasn't always so . . . aware. In my early stand-up years, I was known for making fun of women, specifically the way some of us behave when we're desperate, hungry, or drunk. I felt I had license to do it because I'd lived it; I was in my midtwenties, so my Girl Logic was a little less informed and a lot less evolved than it is today. I thought I had a monopoly on describing nights out that start with aimlessly wandering, jacketless, through the cold to find a bar, sharing a flatbread (so we don't feel too fat); crying Lemon Drop–and–chemical-imbalance-fueled tears; eating terrible 3 a.m. tacos; then waking up for work with last night's makeup still looking sort of good and thinking, "Hey, I can pull this off." This was my life, and the life of most women my age.

But, when I look back, I can't help but question my own harshness. I remember doing one joke where I called a line of drunk girls holding hands to walk through a crowded dance floor a "chain of whores." Surprisingly, women loved it. Fans have even put that joke on T-shirts and worn them to my shows. But if I had to do it over again, I wouldn't have used that word; I was playing on lazy stereotypes. It may pack a punch, but as a constantly evolving woman and comedian, it's my job to look beyond the humor and ask myself if I want to be part of making a derogatory word commonplace. I don't.

Something clicked in April 2015. I was watching television as a male comic publicly shamed a female comic I knew and liked. He called her out by name and made fun of everything from her looks to her personality. His jokes were brutal and unabashed, and the insult to the injury was that they weren't even funny. I found myself growing seriously pissed at his antiwoman labeling and judging and feeling so righteously steadfast that what he was doing was, well, wrong, that I decided to write a rebuttal piece for a popular website. It was like I was on a literary schoolyard, a classmate had been pushed down, and I was the only one who could help her back up. I've had a front-row seat to the constant verbal backlash, write-offs, rumors, and never-ending pissing contests women are subjected to in comedy. It just so happened on that day, for that girl, I could help. Did I change her life, or his? Doubtful, but sometimes you see something shitty happen, and life asks, "Are you gonna stay silent or stand up for what you think is right, even if not everyone hears?"

After my piece went up, my small act of protest lit a fire in me. I realized, as a woman in my thirties, that it was no longer acceptable to use my platform to talk solely about drunk mistakes, nor was that the totality of my existence. It was time to say things onstage that were both funny *and* meaningful. So I used that perspective to write and shape my Netflix special, *Confirmed Kills.* I wanted—and still want—women to arm themselves with confidence, so they'll be that much more prepared the next time someone decides to publicly question why they exist.

I admit I used to make my own negative judgments ("chain of whores") about other women because one of the trickier aspects of Girl Logic is that it affects both how we see ourselves *and* how we see other women. It can destabilize our sense of self, making us compare ourselves to and dismiss other women (more on female competition later in the book). Girl Logic dictates that we should all be confident and empowered, but not too vain or full of ourselves. Otherwise, people will "talk." If you're pretty, you must be stupid; if you're fat, you must not be pretty; but if you lose the weight and show off your body, then you're slutty, showy, annoying, too in shape. (Really, there is an endless list of shitty superlatives that can be applied to anything positive you do.) It's hard to win, either in the real world *or* inside our heads. But women need to find solidarity in our similarity—to recognize that we're all making sense, even when we *aren't* making sense.

When I was growing up in Texas and playing lacrosse in high school, there was a fanatical emphasis on "acting like ladies" when we were representing our school. As if the entire perception of our institution rested on how we conducted ourselves on the field for a sport no one was watching anyway. "Act like ladies"—what does that mean? Be nice? Cordial? Quiet? Faint on a nearby couch? Acting like a man means taking charge and often being tough. Why would I want to be delicate during sports? You see it in professional sports, too— male athletes get paid more, but they also get into fights, yell at refs, and occasionally rape or kill someone. Frankly, I think part of Ronda Rousey's appeal, at the height of her career, was that she broke away from the "shake hands and smile at your opponent," knee-length-skirt model of athleticism that she and other female athletes have been taught to emulate. Instead she was straight-up aggressive; she said what was on her mind, and she could back it up. She was our Dennis Rodman. Serena Williams, too—she's fierce as fuck, and when she isn't happy, she lets it rip, like when she smashed that racket at Wimbledon. Pretty awesome if you ask me.

People don't know how to process female aggression, though. They often mislabel it as negativity. I've definitely been called negative. But . . . why? Because I pace onstage, yell in my jokes, and use my body? Because when I don't like things I call them out? Because I don't back down when it upsets someone who shouldn't have come at me in the first place? To me, negativity is a powerful tool. It reminds us never to get too comfortable. I call myself a realist, though—or maybe a pessimistic optimist. I believe in good, that it will all work out, but I refuse to blindly bump into unnecessary hurdles along the way.

Anyway, point is? More women should be like Ms. Rousey and Ms. Williams: not only strong and indomitable, but also unapologetic and able to back it up. Thankfully there are role models in every field. In comedy we've got Tina Fey, Amy Poehler, Melissa McCarthy, Kate McKinnon, and, hell, all the women of *SNL*. And take a look at Jennifer Saunders, who might be my biggest role model in comedy. All of them are ballsy and unafraid to give an intelligent opinion, commentary, or impression (even if it, God forbid, offends people), play an ugly character, or simply be who they are. In politics we have more and more women like Elizabeth Warren, and in business we have more and more female CEOs at Fortune 500 companies. And yet, despite all of these positive strides and role models, women still unwittingly succumb to micro forms of passivity every day.

We wear heels we can't run in, and dresses we can't breathe in. We don't leave the house without lipstick—gotta make sure your lips look like plump vaginas!—and we do smoky eye makeup because it's "sexy" (even though it makes us look like we just choked on a dick and cried). We try to stay as thin as possible—which also keeps us weak. When you're skinny, you have no body fat; when you have no body fat, you're cold all the time; and when you're cold all the time, you stay inside; and when you stay inside . . . you don't vote. I may be joking about that last part . . . but I'm not totally wrong. Ever stop to think that by keeping women eternally preoccupied with superficialities that we might be missing out on important things in life?

Just imagine if we could consistently direct that crazy mental energy to lift ourselves up, instead of put ourselves down. Because when you are truly secure in yourself—when you can analyze situations and figure out what's best for you, based on *you* and not some preconceived notion of what society expects—then nothing is a threat. (Except mountain lions! There's one constantly loose in my neighborhood; OMG, it ate a neighbor's cat!)

Work It If You Got It

I know I'm not perfect. But despite an insane number of persistently irrational delusions (believing I'll magically wake up tan, understand the subjunctive tense in Spanish, and I'll suddenly be able to wear a flowy tank top without looking pregnant), perhaps the only one I've managed to avoid is the idea that I'm not good enough. Instead, I "suffer" from chronic *over*confidence. It's not that I'm impervious to Girl Logic–fueled self-questioning; I'm as human as the rest of you. It's that, in the best of situations, as I've gotten older, I've learned to channel my GL correctly. I've trained myself to listen to my GL when it's pointing me toward the thing that feels most authentically right for me in the long term, and to ignore it (er, sometimes?) when it's obsessively projecting past fears or rejections onto whatever weirdness is happening in the moment. If I smile at a guy who doesn't return it, I might spin out into a momentary fog of self-doubt, but my heart won't stop beating and my day won't be ruined. If I tell a joke that doesn't get a laugh, so what? There's another joke right after it.

Most decisions we make are fear based: the decision to not take a chance because we're afraid to fail, to not wear an outfit out of fear of looking "bad," to not tell someone we're upset with them because we're scared of confrontation. If you reduce it down, the reality is that of the 10,000 decisions we make every day, very few of them actually matter to your future, and, often, taking the risk will help you gain more than you'll lose. For instance, take this common refrain: "I don't want to text him because the last guy I texted right after a date never texted me back." You're letting your hang-ups from past rejection guide your present decision making. When, in actuality, this is a new guy and a new situation (and a more evolved you; most of us progress as we get older, right?). He either will or won't write you back and, if he doesn't, so what? There is no way you loved him so much that it's gonna hurt for long (despite the fact that you've already tried out what your first name sounds like with his last name, and maybe made a few allowances regarding his lifestyle: "He loves taxidermy, so maybe I could learn to stuff a cute mouse or something"). Truth is, why would you want to date a flake? For God's sake, there are celebrities out there who have killed people, no one cares, and you're still a fan! They're still celebrities! You think the world is gonna notice if you send one dumb e-mail, wear the wrong shoes, or wink at a guy who doesn't like you?

When I don't get a part, I'm shocked (but why was it even between me and Jennifer Hudson in the first place?!). When a guy doesn't call me back, I'm floored. "You have a roommate, use an iPhone for your 'photography,' have an illegitimate child, and *you* aren't calling *me* back? BLOCKED. You are dead to me."

Let me reassure you: my confidence isn't based on any solid irrefutable reason. There's never been anything in my life I truly excelled at aside from comedy, and even that is subjective. I'm not a rapper. I'm not a model. I'm not an athlete. I don't know a good investment when I see one. I have no idea how to wear horizontal stripes correctly. And everyone has insecurities, of course. Me, I hate my thighs—I can never wear the tight pants that fashion wants me to wear because my thighs are not those of a ten-year-old Japanese boy. This torments me daily. So what do I do? I accept the existence of my meaty haunches, and I do squats. I figure if they're gonna be big, let's make them strong.

P.S. Thanks, hip hop culture, for making it easier for women with meat on their bodies to show it off—and for allowing more men to admit they like it. "But stop body-shaming thin girls!" you might cry out, to which I would cry back, "Uh, I *am* thin, and I don't feel shamed. Just slightly annoyed most of the time." Moral of the story? Let our bodies be our bodies; quit studying and labeling them. No one looks at a linebacker and says, "Wow, it's amazing he found a niche spot in the NFL! He's sooooo confident."

Me? I like myself, thighs and all. I know it's sort of de rigueur to hate yourself—"I'm such a hot mess," "I'm so pathetic"—but I won't make jokes like that because they only feed the idea that women should hate themselves. I might say I have the table manners of a starving coyote or that I'm dumb because I think if I just chew Sour Patch kids fast that will, somehow, burn calories. But, deep down, I don't believe there is anything I can't do. If someone told me I had to choreograph a Broadway show, I think I could do it. Part of me secretly thinks I might be the best singer in the world. Delusional? Totally. I like to think high school was all the things I was bad at (math, essays, chemistry, running, and cleaning my room), and now, as an adult, I only have to do things I'm good at. Comedy! Sleeping! Squeezing my dog! Texting back! HUSTLING!

Like I said, I'm not superhuman. I've just grown and changed a lot, and learned how to make my GL work for me instead of against me when it comes to believing in myself and accomplishing my goals.

Anyway, there wasn't that one summer when I got my braces off and came out of my shell, or some life-changing moment when I saw Richard Pryor and thought, "OMG! Comedy is what I'm born to do!" That confidence was just always there. Humor has always been my thing, and before me, it was my parents' thing, and before them it was my grandparents' thing (Thanksgivings are exhausting in our house). It's never let me down. And it's having this Thing that has helped me feel good about myself, even when I was younger and supposed to be writing self-pitying journal entries. (OK fine, I may have written a few of those, too.)

Maybe your Thing is an awesomely exaggerated body part, or an innate ability to sing, or the fact that you don't get squeamish around bodily fluids. (Hi, natural-born ER doc or serial killer!) You can rage against it, but if this thing benefits you and others, why not embrace it? If you're a genius, you will always know the answer. If you're gorgeous, you will always stand out in a crowd. If you're an athlete, you will always be good at sports and evading arrest. And if you're funny, you will always be able to make at least one person in the room laugh, and that's a beautiful and valuable thing.

Quick aside: Some of you folks reading this might be in high school. If so, I want to tell you something: IT REALLY DOES GET BETTER. Unless you're a mean weirdo, you'll most likely end up being praised, as an adult, for the very things you were mocked for in high school. So just hold on a little longer.

There's nothing wrong with knowing how good you are, and there's nothing wrong with taking time to figure that out. One positive aspect of GL is that all its obsessive loops of self-talk can actually help you psych yourself up, be a little prouder, and do your best, no matter what you're doing. Plus, there's nothing wrong with being cocky, especially as a woman. You don't have to be a jerk, but there's nothing wrong with being confident. The next time you look great or do something amazing and someone compliments you, just say, "I know! Thank you!" The only time cockiness doesn't work is when you can't back it up. (It's also worth noting that cockiness is generally considered a "male" trait, named for a male body part that was named after a male chicken: a cockerel. A cockerel's job is to hang out with all the hens and fertilize the eggs and be super aggressive and make a lot of noise. So now you get it. Confident women aren't called snoochy, but maybe we should be. I'm SNOOCHY! NOW TELL ME HOW GOOD I LOOK AND GET OUT OF MY WAY OR I WILL SUFFOCATE YOU.)

Are you still with me? What's that? You've taken this book to the toilet? Gross. Anyway, we were talking about confidence. The true kind that comes from knowing what you're good at and what you're worth. The kind of confidence that gives you the courage to demand what you deserve, even when you're the only one who thinks you deserve it.

The way I figure, if you operate from the assumption that nobody knows anything (which is largely true in show business, as it is in most other industries—except I guess like the CIA; I feel like they know a lot), then one of three things happen when you ask for what you deserve:

One: You ask and they say yes.

Two: You ask and they realize, "Oh wow, didn't realize she was worth that much! She must know something we don't."

Three: They say no, but they walk away knowing you value yourself . . . or that you're wildly off base in your assessment of your value. But the point is, you tried. People will always respect you for trying . . . or think you're annoying, but at least they will remember you. And hey, when you turn out to be a success? They'll look back on it like, "should have given her a chance."

I think a lot of us start out with this sort of confidence and end up losing it somewhere along the way. Our Girl Logic gets stuck in a negative loop and overrides our ability to see ourselves clearly: "If I ask for a raise and they don't give it to me, then I'll feel awkward, and if I feel awkward, then I won't feel comfortable speaking up at work, and I might start to do a bad job and then they'll be like, 'Ew, the nerve on her to ask for a raise when she isn't even good at what she does in the first place.'"

When I was little, I had a strong sense of what I would and would not tolerate, and of what I knew was right (um, even if I was wrong). I thought most other people were wrong, and I wasn't totally wrong to think that. I'm reminded of my first, and only, experience modeling in a childhood fashion show. I was five years old, doing a JCPenney kids' show. They stuck me in an ugly pink and red apron with giant quilted hearts all over it. And white tights. WHITE TIGHTS! QUILTED ANYTHING! I threw a fit. It was ugly. My mother pulled me aside and explained, "These are professionals, and you'll wear what they tell you." I did the stupid fashion show, walked offstage, and ripped the outfit from my body. Right there, in that multipurpose room in the employee section of the Prestonwood Mall, my fashion career was finished. Was I wrong to throw a fit? Maybe. Does anyone here remember a time in children's fashion when pink and red quilted-heart aprons and white tights were chic? NOPE!

That sense that I knew best—because so many other people were clearly inept—has followed me through life. Most people know a lot about, like, three things. Just because someone is in charge doesn't mean they should be, and just because they can express an opinion doesn't mean you should listen to it. Executives create bad shows, politicians do horrible things on purpose, stylists send people out on red carpets wearing garbage trash. Hey, I've been on sets where the makeup artist made my eyebrows so dark I looked like an angry cartoon monkey. I walked on set and my Mexican hairdresser looked at my face and was like, "*changa!*" I've read magazine articles about me with my name misspelled two different ways IN PRINT! Not everyone is in a position of authority because they worked for it. Nope, most people get where they are because the guy ahead of them died, they knew someone, or they simply did a decent enough job long enough that eventually they got promoted.

Is constantly questioning everything and everyone exhausting? Yes! But it's how I'm wired. Is it because I'm Jewish and our religious pastime is sitting around asking, "Why?" Perhaps. Or maybe, when it comes to certain areas of my life, my Girl Logic is stuck in high gear, pushing me constantly to do more, achieve more, checking and double-checking that things are going well. I've seen enough fuckups at my own expense that I've chosen to be on the offense to mitigate any impending poor decisions being made on my behalf. Because, at the end of the day? It's your career, life, face, image, and feelings on the line, and no one should care—or have the power to fuck things up for you—more than you.

On a deeper level, I've always believed I deserved respect. Sure, I had the same nitpicky, self-doubting thoughts every other girl has growing up; my Girl Logic, at times, drove me bonkers when I'm hit with a spin cycle of "What if they don't think I'm cool enough?" and "Should I just stay quiet and see what happens?" GL urges you to demand respect, but it also reminds you that the path to achieving it can be riddled with name calling, doubt, and struggle. I mean, no one wants to be feared and hated. Except maybe Putin. Oh, and Kim Jong . . . any of them.

But, if you think about all the decisions—and all the hardship and pain—that have gone into getting you to this point in your life, is it so insane to think that maybe you've been through enough? Is it so insane to think you deserve to be treated like a worthy human? As I got older and learned more about myself, my GL evolved with me. Fortunately, it changed in a way that helped boost my confidence instead of bring it down. I learned to *expect* people to respect me because I respected myself. Of course, this was also partially instilled by my strong, smart, independent single mother and her "take no crap" New York attitude. (I want to note here that anything good that's happened to me in life is directly because of my mom.)

As a teenager, I was lucky enough to have body confidence. Inexplicably. Well, maybe not that inexplicable: I had boobs. When I was thirteen, my neighbor Aaron threw a pool party. (Aaron was thirteen, too—fortunately this isn't a story about getting molested by a man next door. I know, the second I said "when I was thirteen" and "neighbor," it sounded like it was going that way.) The guys at the party asked the girls to take part in a swimsuit contest. Hey, we were teenagers in Plano, Texas, in the '90s—none of us had a clue what sexism was! Me being me, I jumped at the opportunity. I knew that, with a chest like mine, I was *totally* gonna win the prize: a coveted twenty-dollar Blockbuster gift card.

Don't get me wrong: I wasn't "hot" or anything, though I did have the best *Far Side* T-shirt collection in all the land! But I'd learned that boobs meant something, particularly after my friend Sandra's mother, a life-size 5'10" Barbie doll with long ripples of blonde hair, said to me, "Good God, child, I wish I had your chest!"

What I gleaned from this powerfully inappropriate statement was that the most beautiful woman I knew was jealous of something *I* had. Talk about an ego boost.

Though the other girls might have been able to wear braces and still look cute (what the hell!?), I thought I had the swimsuit competition on lock. And yet, no sooner had we lined up, my grown-woman chest all pigeon-puffed out, that Aaron declared Angela, my Sun-In blonde nemesis (who didn't know she was my nemesis, and, honestly, I would have been so excited if she'd wanted to hang out with me), the winner. "Aaron obviously has a crush on Angela—that's why she won," I seethed to myself as I threw a Yaga shirt over my Esprit tankini.

Truth be told, Angela was prettier than me, at least by Texas standards: cute nose, a perpetual tan, and the au courant haircut—the "Rachel"—that went on to be mocked 'round the world. As for me, I had blonde curls that broke at my temples and sort of hovered above my head, like a halo of fuzz. I never "did" my hair, save the one time I did like ten braids to try to resemble the yellow-sweater-wearing version of Alanis Morissette in the "Ironic" video.

I'd inherited my dad's prominent snout—a nose that trickled down my nana's bloodline and had been dubbed the "Chinsky Hook." What young girl doesn't dream of having a nose named for a Polish snaring device?

This is the part of the book where you're blessed with the realization that I had a nose job at eighteen. I'm Jewish! And no one has ever asked me about my surgery, so it was obviously a good one. But was I insecure about my nose? More than anything. I would sit in class and hide my profile because I thought it was so hideous. No one made fun of me except for one kid who called me "Rhino Nose." (And I'll never forget it because I had a crush on him. In hindsight, he wasn't even that cute, which made him more attainable . . . and he still thought I was ugly! What a punch in the hook.) I didn't *feel* ugly, though; I just knew I had an ugly nose and the universe had made a mistake.

Now, back to the pool and back to me always knowing I'm right and that the universe is out to get me. What infuriated me was that the poolside competition wasn't a face contest; it was supposed to be about how your body looked in a swimsuit. THOSE WERE THE RULES! NOT FACE, BODY! And yet! Right there in that Texas backyard I had my first foray into

the cruel world of superficial judgments and began to understand that life wasn't fair. (Oddly, I hadn't fully absorbed that
lesson when my parents got divorced, which didn't faze me.)

I don't know where Angela is now, but I'm sure that early
confirmation of her hotness has served her just fine in this life
and that she's grown up to be a wonderful nurse or receptionist
or benefits administrator or whatever in fill-in-the-blank,
Texas. Probably with carloads of good-looking, All-American,
perpetually bronzed kids. (I just searched for her on Facebook—turns out she went to Stanford and now runs a huge
charity. Wow, I totally misjudged her. Wait, aha! She *does* have
good-looking children! SEE? I CALLED IT!)

Thankfully, the jury-rigged bikini contest didn't scar me too
badly, and I came to believe that I was somewhere *just above
average* on the attractiveness scale. It has since occurred to me
that without the marvels of modern medical advances like acne
cream and braces and surgery and Instagram filters, most of us
would walk around looking like absolute she-rats all the time.
Sometimes I wonder, if I were a peasant in the 1600s, what
would I have looked like? Cystic acne, Chinsky Hook, and
snaggleteeth running wild—I'd probably be married off to a
hog farmer or perhaps hung as a witch.

I got my aforementioned nose job right before I went to
college. At first I told my friends that something had fallen on
my face, and everyone believed it. This was Dallas, not Long
Island. No one in my school got nose jobs, so it seemed plausi-
ble that a gigantic wooden Martha's Vineyard "FRESH FISH

HERE" sign from my parents' living room could land on my face. Plus, we were all off to college; no one else had time to think about my nose.

All I can tell you is that I woke up from the surgery, eyes black and blue, with a broken swollen piggy nose, so sensitive I'd cry if you touched it with your pinky. I looked in the mirror and, through my bleary eyes, realized that I'd never felt prettier or more normal. That was my standard of beauty. If you have a big nose and you keep it, that's awesome. My point is, *I* didn't like something about *myself,* so I changed it. I didn't mock other girls with bumpy noses, and I never hated girls who had perfect noses. Insecurities are a personal thing: you should handle them and not project them on anyone else.

To me, a little plastic surgery is no different from losing a little weight or changing your hair color. If tweaking one thing will help you feel better about yourself, why not do it? Just know that deciding to alter a superficial "flaw" won't necessarily fix whatever emotional weirdness you might be holding inside about said flaw. Tons of fat people who've lost weight via natural means, surgery, or anything else still say they feel fat inside. Plenty of people who change their faces still don't feel attractive. And while I don't struggle with many self-esteem issues, there have been and will continue to be plenty of times I've flat-out decided, "I'm not pretty enough for that guy." Attraction is animalistic, not merit based. And people will, either out of politeness or genuine shock, scoff at you if you say you aren't pretty or another woman is prettier. But just because someone is more attractive than me doesn't mean I don't think I deserve to live. I just call 'em like I see 'em.

I'll admit it: I think I'm pretty now. (Some of the time, anyway. When I'm at my best, doing stand-up, I'm not pretty. In any action shots of me onstage, I'm never making a decent face or not hunched over like a Party Goblin.) But rejection always hurts, and the younger it happens to you, the more of a mark it makes. I'll never forget being fourteen, at summer camp, and thinking this one kid was cute. We were all going to sit in a circle, and I went and sat next to him, quietly. Everyone was milling about so he got up and moved, and so I waited a few seconds and moved, too. When I sat down next to him again—again not making eye contact or saying a word—he looked at me and said, "Stop trying to sit next to me." Like I was some hideous fart beast who kept licking him. Ever ready with a verbal quip, I snipped, "Uh, I'm not." When he moved again, I dared not follow. Small as that was, for years afterward I felt I shouldn't look at boys because I was offending them.

As for me, my own self-confidence stems not just from the notion that I am a good person worthy of love and respect but that I am, well, just a tiny bit better than some people. I KNOW, I know, that's a lofty statement—one that could easily be misread, misinterpreted, or simply make me sound like a big bitch. But honestly, it just boils down to being a decent person who does decent things.

I hate when, in an argument between women, the conversation devolves to, "So you think you're *better* than everyone?"

and the other girl reflexively quacks back, "Oh my God, who, me? Noooooo, of course not!"

If you tried that with me, the conversation would go like this. . . .

THEM: "So you think you're better than everyone?"
ME: "No, not everyone. Just some! OK, and maybe you!"

In a perfect world we would all have a little societal Yelp rating floating above our heads to indicate to others, right off the bat, whether we're garbage people or not. Wouldn't it be great if you could meet someone and immediately see their five-star review that reads, "Stacey gives to charity, adopted an animal, is a great friend, and cares for her grandma"? Then you could compare her to Todd, who has two stars but *seemed so cool.* You'd read, "Todd lives off his parents, deliberately gave his last girlfriend chlamydia, has a coke problem, and once Postmated a bottle of Jack because he didn't feel like walking downstairs to 7-Eleven. Oh, and he vapes. Competitively." Side note: between the writing and publishing of this book, a *Black Mirror* episode came out with a similar idea about human ratings. I just want you to know that I had it first! Five stars!

Yup, most people are *the worst.* Not you, of course—you obviously have great taste and humor, not to mention you're reading an actual book, which is more than I can say for most people. (Fine, I admit it—we tried to condense the book into five silly memes about puppies sleeping, but I felt like my message was getting lost.)

And Work It If You Don't Got It

Before I won *Last Comic Standing,* before I accomplished something unique, nothing in my life suggested I was going to be anything special to anyone besides my mother, Ronnie. I wasn't great at school—a B and C student—but my saving grace was that I really put in a solid effort, so in challenging subjects that only Stephen Hawking could understand, like Algebra 101, the teachers loved me because I tried *so, so* hard.

Just kidding.

My secret was that I spent most of my time looking like I was trying. I'd meet with the teacher, do extra credit—anything I could to show I was going through the motions of learning (but wasn't actually learning, because, for me, MATH IS BORING AND IMPOSSIBLE).

On tests, I lived to hear, "Oh you were so close, and I *know* you were struggling with this and I noticed you wrote down the right answer and then erased it, so I'll give you half a point."

Success! I scratched my way to a mediocre GPA one pity-point at a time. I did the studying, I had the tutors, in middle school I cheated by storing information in my TI-83. I took the after-school brushup classes, but it wasn't clicking. (I'm speaking about math and chemistry here; any other subject was fine. To this day, I can still recite the Middle English prologue of *The Canterbury Tales.*)

But there comes a point in your academic career when you have to surrender to the fact that you just don't—and never will—understand math. Then you have to let that cold, hard reality manifest itself in your GPA as it will.

I knew I'd thrive if I could just move past the school thing and enter the real world, where talent and creativity matter (LOL) instead of the blind memorization of theorems and chemical equations. It would all start with college. There, they would see me for the endlessly creative and magical creature I was! I would make my art, be lauded for my humor, and shamelessly wear pajamas to class and easily gain ten pounds my freshman year . . . and sophomore year. . . . Whatever, it's hard to make healthy choices when the FOOD IS ALWAYS IN THE DINING HALL! A 24-HOUR YOGURT BAR? ARE YOU FUCKING KIDDING ME?! WHAT KIND OF A SCRUMPTIOUS HEAVEN-HELL IS THIS!?

Back to my fun fantasy world. My Girl Logic was part of the engine pushing me to disregard the crap I'd learned in high school, like, "play sports and join clubs you don't care about because other kids do it, plus it'll look good on your application." My GL kept whispering that, deep down, the creativity I'd been fostering would simply *have to be* rewarded because IT WAS MY TIME. I thought, "This is the path for all funny people; no one understands you and then one day . . . YOU'RE FAMOUS!" First step toward that? College!

Could I have skipped that step and moved right to LA at eighteen? Yeah, but, with no training, skills, or know-how (also, the fact that not going to college was just not an option in my wildest imagination), I can tell you for a fact that I would have ended up making a lot of money doing something shady, like managing the HR department at Vivid Video, all while justifying to my parents, "I'm nowhere near the porn—it's a normal company with a great insurance package!" But to stay creative I would end up doing long-form improv in Burbank on weekends, and my troupe would have some "hilarious" name like Hot Dog Time Machine. No, college was the way.

I would go there, and my teachers and fellow students wouldn't even notice how bad I was with trig or how low my standardized test scores were—they'd sense something deeper in me. They'd spot my raw talent and pick up on the fact that I had the heart of a great comedic artiste. I would head off to film school and move to LA and become a famous funny person, the breezy celebrity who claims her airplane "essentials" are Hermès scarves, Valentino loafers, and canned placenta dust (for the protein, of course). So I visited, researched, and sent personal essays to the best film schools in the country:

NYU
SARAH LAWRENCE
BARD
SYRACUSE
VASSAR
USC
ITHACA
BU
UT
CHAPMAN
POMONA
EMERSON COLLEGE
NORTHWESTERN

I was rejected by every single one of them.

Not even wait-listed! I couldn't even hang on to the possibility that the kid ahead of me would die or have a hallucinogenic-mushroom-fueled meltdown and let me nab his spot. My confidence, however, remained unwavering. I couldn't grasp why these schools didn't want me. So what if I came in at far below average on all the traditional litmus tests of academic aptitude? I had MOXIE! And I used words like "MOXIE"! But . . . nope. It wasn't enough. This time, there would be no half points awarded for perceived effort. Drat!

Of course, the truth was that I hadn't *earned* entrance to those schools, and I was delusional to think I'd get in. My fantasy-driven GL had been pushing me in a positive direction, of course—deciding to go to college and pursue the arts was obviously a good idea. But in the excitement of pursuing my dream, I decided that inherent creativity would have to override things like grades, athletic achievement, and academic ability. Sure, I'd tested into a competitive prep school in Dallas, but I had a horrific SAT score (sorry, I already told you I had a nose job, you don't get to know my shitty SAT score—that number dies with me), took no honors classes, and I was JV on every sport until I did lacrosse, where there weren't enough of us for JV *and* varsity so we were just one team. I dropped out of the Stock Market Club three weeks in because it was nothing like the movie *Wall Street*. And I couldn't be in the Spanish Club because, even after six years of the language, I was still speaking in *solamente* present tense (though I knew tons of random vocab words about airplanes and vegetables).

Luckily, I'd applied to the University of Kansas in case hell froze over, which was, as I would come to find out, exactly how locals describe the winter weather there. I soaked up KU for a year, had a blast, and then transferred to Emerson College in Boston. That's right, on my second try, I got into Emerson and felt validated. Years later, as I accepted Emerson's Young Alumni Achievement Award for winning *Last Comic Standing*, I would tell the students that "just because they don't see it in you, doesn't mean it's not there." I doubt anyone involved with that award knew Emerson's administration had rejected me the first time around.

I also want to point out that I was granted that award for winning *another* award based on skills I had acquired through a lifetime of rejection. All because, before I was anybody, I thought I was somebody.

Given all that, it's probably not surprising that I became a stand-up comic—a job that requires a surplus of confidence to combat all the rejection and wheel spinning of show business. I was surprised, though, that before long the media (media at my level being bloggers, morning-show DJs, other comics whispering, etc.) had labeled me a "hot" girl in comedy—another moniker I hadn't really earned. "She's hot," people would vomit out. Sometimes followed by, " . . . so she can't be funny." Or worse, "She's hot, so I'm going to be a complete shit to her because I'm still butt-hurt that the prom queen didn't date me in high school." Out of nowhere I had this new identity that came with a false perception that my life had been easy, that I'd always been the favored pretty girl who got everything she wanted. Motherfuckers, funny was all I ever had.

So sad, huh? "Oh, people thought you were sooooo pretty, boo hoo." I'll liken it to this: What if you had been heavy your whole life and then you moved to, say, Milwaukee, and suddenly everyone around you was twice your size? Sounds great, right? Sure, until people start calling you a bitch because, to them, you're thin, and you're left thinking, "What the hell? What did I do to you? I don't deserve this. I've dealt with shit, too!"

On the road, one of the necessary evils we comedians encounter is the morning radio DJ. Morning DJs—thoughtful cultural commentators that they are—love to say things like, "So, is doing stand-up hard as a hot chick? Are you single? What's your favorite sex position?" Who asks that of a stranger at 7 a.m.? What's that got to do with me letting you know I'm at the Giggle Bucket this weekend?

"Is it hard being hot and being on the road? Is it hard being hot and ordering dinner?" I was sitting there with no celebrity boyfriends, no pageants, no trophies or modeling credits, and bags under my eyes, and I'm supposed to talk about what life has been like for a "hot girl"? Go fuck yourselves. "You know what is hard?" I wanted to tell them. "Running on three hours of sleep while being interviewed by a failed open mic-er with an inferiority complex. I'm trying to sell tickets! I'm sorry your dick isn't everything you'd hoped it would be! SEE ME AT THE FUNNY BONE THIS FRIDAY!"

Because I'm blonde and outspoken, people assume I've always been the "mean girl," the head cheerleader. But those kinds of assumptions encapsulate a whole other aspect of Girl Logic: having to deal with *other women's* GL. For example, a girl who was mocked for being dorky in high school might grow up, look at me, and write me off, thinking, "I'm not even gonna bother; she's just going to be mean to me. All blonde girls were and are terrible." It's a classic GL loop: turning something that happened in the past into a negative expectation that will eternally color your present and future.

Whatever, though—I'm not going to write a book about how being an upper-middle-class white girl who had her college paid for has been hard. Black, white, brown, fat, thin, ugly, pretty, molested . . . everybody has their shit, and everybody has stories about how they overcame it (or didn't; some people write books from prison, I guess). Did I have a hard life? I had my struggles, but I've never been discriminated against because of my skin color, I've never been overweight, I've never gone without food, I've never been abused. My objective isn't for you to pity me. I only aim to tell my story.

And let me share something with you that I didn't do much thinking on until I was writing this book. For my whole life, I struggled to make friends. I changed schools five times between first grade and high school, and I always had to adjust to new social rules. Everywhere I went, people already had their cliques, so I was constantly fighting to be included. My mother showed me a letter I wrote to "God" in the second grade where

I asked him to make all the girls in my class fall asleep so I could whisper to them that they should invite me to their sleepovers. I think having a sense of self and being hyperaware from a young age made me. . . . Ah, fuck it; I think it was my nose.

But not being included hurt. And that sense of exclusion leaves kids thinking they aren't important and are easily forgotten. Which brings us to my present-day dilemma. My biggest fear in life (aside from being kidnapped and having my mouth duct-taped shut and being unable to communicate that I can't breathe through my nose) is feeling like I never existed. After high school and college, it felt like I was walking through life alone. Though I still have a few close friends from my younger days, I'm not in touch with 99 percent of the people I went to college or high school with. Depending on what else was going on at the time, my GL would either tell me to withdraw completely or to keep reaching out, but I usually didn't because I felt too . . . disregarded. As a result, I've created a relationship with my fans in which I get back a lot of what I've always needed: not only acceptance but being wanted in the first place.

In a way, my independence born out of rejection has been a good thing. Because of my past, I'm super sensitive to people feeling included, and whether I'm at a party or at work, I'm always the first to say, "Come sit with us." Do I love competition? I do. In fact, I hate losing more than I enjoy winning. But my objective is never to make someone feel like they're wrong for wanting to be part of a group. I think that's why my comedy is so inclusive. I want people to come to my shows and feel that someone understands them.

But when someone does make unfounded assumptions about you right off the bat, it almost never has to do with anything you actually did. How could it? There was a club I didn't play for years because the booker decided she just . . . didn't like whatever little she knew about me. Maybe she just didn't like me? Maybe she hated female comics? Who knows? But I couldn't change her mind.

To be fair, we all do this kind of projecting, at least sometimes. When I was sixteen, a girl from Australia broke my best friend's heart, so for years I hated Australians. Rather than realizing this was immensely ignorant, I thought I was "ride or die." Loyalty to the Point of Stupidity should be plastered on my tombstone. (P.S. Australians are not only the happiest, nicest people ever, but they're also almost all hot.)

The worst, though, is how this plays out with men. Every now and again guys are shitty to me; they seem to forget that I'm not, in fact, one of the girls who wouldn't go out with them in high school. Once I went out for drinks with a dorky—but cute and smart—writer, and afterward, lo and behold, he didn't call. It happens. A week later, he texted, "How does it feel?" Not sure if he was telling me he loved D'Angelo or if he was sending another girl a sexual text, I typed back, "What?" His response: "Being rejected."

DUDE? PLEASE DO SOCIETY A FAVOR AND GO LIVE WITH RACCOONS IN A FOREST.

Now, obviously, he is an insane person, and that is an extreme example. But that sort of "I'll show her" attitude can quite easily escalate into "I'm bringing an AK-47 to the workplace tomorrow because women won't fuck me." Naturally, I blocked him and then talked shit about him to my friends. I had to get *something* satisfying out of that date.

So, to all the dudes out there actively seeking a girl to be angry at, here's a bit of breaking news: I was never a cheerleader. I was actually the school mascot (a giant hornet—I had a stinger and a giant head, and I was glorious). I was not the homecoming queen, I was in our school improv group. I skipped basketball to do the yearly fall musicals, I didn't drink, and for about a year I attended raves with my best friend, Michelle, solely because we loved the dancing. (I know it would be cooler to say were candy kids who loved ecstasy, but for us, it was really just about escaping the banality of playing flip cup with our friends every weekend.)

I am nothing like the girl who rejected you. My parents divorced when I was seven, my father moved away, and when I was eight a malamute bit my face ON THANKSGIVING. That part isn't really germane to the story, it's just kinda crazy. Point is, my life hasn't been all hand jobs and lollipops. More like rejection, sidelines, and *some* hand jobs when I was too full from dinner to have sex.

Mental Makeover

I've always thought the cliché shouldn't be "what doesn't kill you makes you stronger"; it should be "what doesn't kill you should have tried harder, and just leaves you kind of annoyed." Because I get annoyed a lot. I'm annoyed right now, and I'm not even sure why. I get frustrated with almost everything: people, situations, societal expectations . . . gravity, pedestrians, any shirt with the shoulders cut out . . . and the fact that no matter how hard I try, I can never pick a good book on my own. I somehow always end up with something about witchcraft or World War II.

And I get *really* annoyed when I think I'm being undervalued by others, which happens often when you think you're a ten (or at least an eight who reads a lot and does squats) and other people are too dumb to see it. Friends who set you up with a loser, a boss who won't give you the job you want, or a director who won't give you a chance; all are iterations of someone not smart enough to realize your value.

Evaluating your worth based on the opinions of others is a dangerous trap. The perpetual juggling act of trying to process everyone else's assumptions about you—assumptions that are often incorrect—is as exhausting as it is useless. I'm the first to admit it's tough to stay strong when your Girl Logic kicks in and nudges you into nitpicking over why that new friend is blowing you off and what HER reaction to you might mean about your other friends, and the friends you had when you were six, and your future friendability (or lack thereof).

To be a woman who thrives, you have to pinpoint what's good about you and let the confidence in that guide you. Whether it's a stunning sense of humor, a brilliant brain, or a body chiseled from fucking marble, hopefully you feel worthy of attention, love, and acceptance—and when you don't get it, fuckin' right you're pissed. Think about anytime you've gone on a date and it was good (not delusional good, good like it was clear both parties were having fun), and the person never communicated with you afterward. You're left thinking, "I'm pretty great, how is this person not seeing this?" Then you immediately take a sexy picture and post it on Instagram, hoping they're secretly stalking you. No? Just me? Come on, you know they're lookin'.

Point is, I don't think it's possible to be overly confident, especially as a woman. So let the losers hate, and be the best at whatever it is you do, without apologizing. After all, which surgeon would you choose to perform your surgery—the one who says, "This is going to go incredibly and you'll be back to work in no time," or the one who admits, "I'm not quite sure how this will pan out; let's just hope I don't fuck up, LOL."

Holding your head high in the face of all life throws at you can be tough. We live in an era when not only is being a feminist hard, but being judged on what *kind* of feminist you are is a given. But honestly, confidence is kinda . . . everything. Your GL might sometimes be the devil on your shoulder, whispering that you're not good enough. But more often than not, she's actually your ally—trying to help you remember past patterns and future pitfalls. Give her some credit every now and then; she deserves it. She's just trying to help you enjoy your life!

One of my favorite quotes ever is from Jon Stewart: "I'm not going to censor myself to comfort your ignorance." Maybe the girl version should be: "I'm not going to downplay my strengths so you feel less shitty about your own shortcomings." Shout it from the mountaintops, then come down from that mountain because dudes can see up your skirt (unless you're into that, which is totally cool).

2

Case Clothed

Let's face it: most women's clothing seems designed to make us feel horrible, no matter what size we are. I can't count the number of normal outfits I've tried on in a dressing room that ended with the salesperson sniffing at me, "Oh, you're not supposed to wear a bra with that." Are you fucking kidding me, Skyler? Am I eighteen? Is it 1969?

Clothing-related Girl Logic can lead you on a roller coaster ride full of, well, lots of downs and only a few ups. You may be innocently trying on clothes for fun, but if your GL goes off the rails, you could be left in tears, not only hating your body but your job, hair, best friend, and that one bitch who works at the juice place who never smiles at you! All because of one pair of jeans that said "size 6" but we all know were really a 0 and solely there to make you feel like a POORLY SHAPED LOSER WHO

WILL NEVER FIND LOVE OR BE HAPPY BECAUSE THE UNIVERSE HATES YOU.

The reason Girl Logic and clothing are so combustible together is because clothes are a physical expression of how we want to appear—or *think* we should appear—to the outside world. A lot of our ideas about what we should be wearing are absorbed via osmosis from the fashion world: an industry built on making women hate themselves. We inadvertently buy into the aesthetic that dictates all women should be 5'10″ and 105 pounds every time we pick up a magazine or click an Instagram link to a fashion blogger (the caption always being "Obsessed with this look"). We're passively encouraged to criticize, compare, and nitpick our own bodies, so when our fashion options meet our Girl Logic, our clothing choices often veer into the irrational.

This isn't because women are stupid, of course—it's just aspiration gone awry. That's the only reason otherwise rational women will think OF COURSE paying too much money for jeans so tight your vagina looks like it's in a choke hold is a good idea; I mean, *Vogue* said so. Here's a tip: if you can't sit down or normally function in an item of clothing, don't buy it. You'll wear it once, get PTSD, and then fear it every time you stumble across it in your closet. I feel that way about a pair of white rag & bone skinny jeans. Every year I wear them once, hate them, and then bury them in the closet (they're rb, I'm not throwing them out) only to rediscover them next summer. Like unearthing a long forgotten treasure, I then grab them from under a pile of heels on the closet floor, and think "this year fashion will be mine!" Oh wait, they're still a size 24 and I can't even zip 'em. Back to the closet floor you go.

Of course, I'm no fashionista. (In fact, I hear the term "fashionista," and I automatically think of some heavily high-lighted fashion blogger from Ohio pairing a J. Crew sweater with a bebe bracelet and "making it work.") Although I've never been super into clothes, the fact remains: fashion matters—both in how women perceive themselves and in how others see us.

Take men, for instance. They're visual creatures, we're constantly told. So we're expected to dress in a certain "appealing" way to get their attention. No man has ever approached a swamp monster in a floppy hat and said, "Excuse me—you're hideous, but you look like you might enjoy Madden 17, BBQ, and light nipple play. Can I buy you a steak dinner?"

Unfortunately, because we're under the influence of both modern media and outdated cultural standards, women's happiness is often contingent on the amount and type of attention we get from men. I've posted thousands of Instagram pictures, some "pretty" and some veering toward the aforementioned swamp monster. When I post a picture of myself walking through an airport at 6 a.m. and some idiot decides to comment that I "look tired," it saddens me. Not because my feelings are hurt (fuckin' right I'm tired, I got up at 3 a.m. to fly across the country to stand for two hours) but because my purpose on this earth is to make people laugh, not to turn them on. If men keep putting out such benumbingly stupid observations, at this rate we're *never* gonna colonize Mars.

Anyway, back to clothes. Let's pretend for a second that we are leaving the house and going somewhere non-airport-related. Yes, we are putting a pause on our daily agenda of coffee-sipping, peanut-butter-spoon-licking, Facebook refreshing, and dog-song-singalong-ing to venture out and be great in the world. And during this effort, we might want to look and feel our self-confident, attractive best. Well, prepare for a battle, because if you want to feel good and look great in your clothes, you're gonna have to fight for it.

Every woman has gone through this in a dressing room. You walk into the store feeling fine, but after a few try-ons and rounds of "Why are these size 8s not fitting me when I'm usually a 6? How am I not able to squeeze my calves into these jeans that are supposed to be, like, 72 percent stretch?" You actually start to feel . . . uglier. There must be some sort of biochemical Girl Logic reaction caused by incandescent lighting hitting your fat cells, because they actually seem to *multiply* as you're trying on jeans. Most of my shopping trips end with exhaustion, depression, and a resigned, "Is there a Sbarro around here?"

No matter how in shape you are—fashion companies will make it clear you are the *wrong* shape. Your arms are too fat for this type of tank, your legs are too long for these jeans. As a woman, whatever you are, you're always somehow wrong. There are whole brands out there inadvertently dedicated to letting you know your body type isn't *their* body type.

True story: a friend's sister applied to an Urban Outfitters. She's nineteen. She's adorable and a little curvy, but no more than the average college freshman at a big state school. When her application was rejected, she asked the manager why she wasn't hired because she wanted to improve on anything she could. He told her, "You don't have the right body type for our brand."

Look, I get it; if you are selling athletic apparel, you want your "team members" to reflect the image you want your brand to project. But, the last time I checked, you didn't need 2 percent body fat to hock babydoll dresses left over from 1995, coffee table books about Instagram cats, and bacon-scented candles. Also? There were about a hundred ways he could have rejected her that didn't involve crushing the self-esteem of a kid just trying to get a retail job. As if girls bigger than size 6 don't want to buy cute clothes, too. I hope he hangs himself with a graphic tee.

Something else that can make the shopping process more excruciating is a bad saleswoman. If she casually lies that you "look awesome" as she walks past while you're posing in your pulled silk skort onesie, OR if she's exponentially hotter than you, run. Do not trust her with your money or your self-esteem. I learned this the hard way recently when I had to buy a dress for an event and found the salesgirl standing around pouting, looking far more beautiful than me. Like, model hot. Not the kind of model your weird college friend pretends to be on Facebook, either—not the kind who sits on vintage cars, does burlesque, and sometimes sells Xanax. No, this salesgirl was 5′9″, 120 pounds, with long blonde hair and wide-set eyes and legs like Karli Kloss and a baby giraffe gave birth to . . . a baby giraffe. She was a stunning version of a praying mantis.

I just wanted to watch *her* try on clothes! And she was so nice. The more I joked and the more she laughed, the more beautiful she got, and the more I felt like the ugly court jester trying on leggings to please her majesty! She kept bringing me "cool" outfits that ended up making me feel unattractive and out of date. "Try this! It's a sleeveless turtleneck dress with a zipper up the front." A whole zipper running up the front? Did we get this from a Body Glove trunk show? No? OK, what time should I meet the other "gals" at Cache?

When she laughed, a beautiful white dove flew from her mouth. "It's all about attitude, girl," she beamed. I was like, "Cool! But my attitude would improve if I didn't have the most beautiful mantis-like woman trying to style me like I'm fifty and 'getting back on the dating scene.'" I left and bought some new makeup instead. And maybe some Chick-fil-a.

In some ways, the biggest enemy modern women face is fashion. OK fine—maybe rape, murder, cancer, heart disease, and domestic violence come first—THEN all that bullshit you see everywhere from your favorite magazines, to Instagram posts, websites, and your local mall mannequins. Regardless, it feels an awful lot like the fashion and beauty industry's sole purpose is to make us crave a lifestyle we don't have and make us hate our bodies in the process. I'm not a conspiracy theorist, but I firmly believe those industries thrive solely on women's insecurities.

That said, turning to celebrities like the Kardashians for fashion or beauty inspiration makes zero sense—even THEY don't look like that. Hyperplumped lips, padded butts, breasts pouring out of everything. . . . When and how did our Girl Logic start insisting that we need to stack up to walking, talking sex dolls? You may be wondering if, by saying this, I am shaming women who *naturally* look like them. My answer is no, because let's be honest—"real" women who look like the Kardashians are few and far between. Am I contradicting myself from that page in the first chapter where I said I was OK with plastic surgery? Nope. My personal take on surgery is if it's a corrective procedure that will help you feel more confident in who you are, do it. But . . . NOT if it makes you resemble a breathing blow-up doll with lips that look like a huge wet vagina.

I mean, when it comes to overly enhanced lips and asses, I just don't believe women are doing it "for themselves"—I think it's so men will get hard when they look at them. Are women merely capitalizing on their sexual power over men? Maybe. But then we should be honest about that. It's not like there's a woman out there who claims, "When I flew Spirit Air the seats were so hard, my butt did nothing to cushion my tailbone; but after I got these butt implants, well, I was flyin' high! What a practical, and not at all sexual, medical procedure!" But, at the end of the day, who cares, right? Let women do what they want. No one wants to look or feel old, but maybe the inevitability of age wouldn't be such a crushing blow if we stopped blaming women for aging in the first place. I mean, Jennifer Aniston is over forty-seven years old, and tabloids only *recently* stopped accusing her of being pregnant. Do the fucking math, people.

Having a big butt, of course, is something that's been cele-
brated in black culture and demonized in white culture. If a
black guy told me I had a fat ass, I'd know it was a compliment.
If a white guy said it, I'd know it was an insult. That actually
happened to me at a bakery in New York. (I even have an Instagram video of it!) I was with a friend, debating my friend's
assertion that "even the sexiest woman isn't sexy all the time."
(I disagreed because I know Sofia Vergara is sexy all the time. I
don't have surveillance footage to prove it. Yet.) There was a
Puerto Rican woman behind the counter, so I flipped the camera on her and said, "What about you, do you think a woman
can be sexy all the time?" She replied, "You're a white girl with
a fat ass; I think you can be whatever the hell you wanna be."
Totally inappropriate way to talk to a customer, but I knew she
meant it as a compliment. Guess what? Big butts are in style
and, white girls? You can try, but black girls (and Latina girls
and Armenian girls) beat us on this front. Now most of us are
doomed to watch from the sidelines, ass-less. Frankly, given the
amount that black women have been discounted in our society,
I think this is more than fair.

Anyway, back to shopping. Chronically envisioning—and
shopping for—a fantasy life that isn't yours is, again, all about
indulging your Girl Logic. It happens to me, too. Just this
morning I saw an ad with a sullen model wearing untied Doc
Martens and a black choker and I thought, quite seriously,
"Maybe tomorrow I'll wake up in the '90s and finally get to be
the lead singer in that punk band I never started because my
mom was always there for me."

Of course, Girl Logic isn't all bad when it comes to clothes. Sometimes your GL can nudge you to take a risk with your style, like a cat eye or fishnets! And lo and behold, sometimes that risk pays off. For instance, I remember having to get dressed once for a women's comedy event. Now, knowing the room would be filled with women, my GL kicked in. I couldn't dress sexy. First of all, why? I was (A) doing stand-up and (B) doing it in front of a room of women; who was I trying to turn on? Women all want acceptance and sisterhood, sure, but that doesn't mean we're above scrutinizing each other's bodies and the outfits on them. Would there be some women there who might love me more if I wore a skimpy tank top and tight jeans? Maybe. But I didn't want to take the chance and be written off for dressing too sexy or, worse, have anyone be distracted from my words.

So I asked my neighbor Bonnie to help me shop. She's a mother and a casting director. She's older than me, and she's been living in Hollywood twenty years longer than I have. She picked out a pair of Alexander Wang gaucho pants. As a creature with muscular legs, I've had bad experiences with anything that stops at my ankle; that just makes my legs look thicker and shorter. My GL whispered that I must stay the hell away from those gaucho pants, given the trauma of my prior ankle-pants experiences. Bonnie told me to shut up and try them on. To this day, they are the best pair of pants I own. Why should I not allow myself to wear an entire subset of pants simply for fear of not looking like a leggy model, which I could never look like in the first place, no matter what type of pants I am wearing? EMBRACE THE HAUNCH!

Anyway, I did the show, looked amazing, and felt . . . expensive. Then, a couple months later on the *Tonight Show*, I fully regressed and wore a dress so tight it actually *cut my armpits*. Whatever, live and learn. I also want to note that I love trashy clothes: cutoff shorts, leg warmers, mesh tops, Lycra miniskirts, fingerless gloves, thigh-high socks, full-length mesh body stockings—obviously I can't wear this garbage without looking like I'm going to an '80s-themed rave, but I see these items in windows, and, for a brief second, my GL fantasizes about a world where I can wear all this junk and still maintain my dignity.

All our false fashion beliefs kinda make sense, though, "If you build it, they will come," right? For women, it's "If you wear this, it WILL HAPPEN." Who among us hasn't spotted some sexy, ridiculous mesh body stocking or something and immediately been flooded with images of the perfect Saturday night flashing on an endless loop through their brain: late-night make-out sessions, tapas without bloating, drinks without puking, dancing without sweating—a night that *obviously* wouldn't come to pass if this one magic top weren't in the equation? Women routinely buy clothes for events that haven't happened yet: vacations that aren't planned, red carpets they haven't been invited to. That's Girl Logic for you. We shop for perceived inevitabilities: unnamed future fashiony funerals, awards shows, flashy polo-game fund-raisers in the Hamptons. ("Oh! Good thing I bought navy jeans, riding boots, and an Anne Fontaine fitted white blouse for just such an occasion!") I once bought a pair of five-inch cork wedge sandals just in case I wanted to look like a circa-2000 Steve Madden cartoon at a beach party that I hadn't been invited to. YET.

I don't delude myself, though—high heels and ridiculous wedges are worn for one reason alone: to make women look thinner, taller, and hotter to dudes. Duh. I mean, men like big tits, right? So women get breast implants, push-up bras, boob bronzers, the list goes on. And please don't tell me getting implants was something you "did for yourself." Highlights, nose jobs, breast implants, tans . . . no one would bother with any of that stuff if they lived alone in a forest. That's why all girls love raggedy old sweatpants, T-shirts, and "home clothes"—they're cozy, comfy, and easy, and we wear them in secrecy when we're not worried about impressing anyone (or when we've been dating someone long enough).

Back to boobs now. Any girl who was "blessed" with large ones at an early age can tell you: there will never, ever, be anything out there for you when it comes to dressing that chest, and sometimes it'll feel like absolutely no one understands your painful plight because you have something everyone else seems to want.

By age fifteen, I was a 32DD. And BTW, it's utterly useless to have *that* much boob at *that* age. No boy knows what to do with them (not that any boy was touching them), no clothes fit right, and they just get in the way during sports. While all my friends were running around in perky B-cup floral bras from Victoria's Secret or Abercrombie, my mom was hauling me across town to a jarringly well-lit old-lady store called Loretta's Intimate Apparel. (The name Loretta alone confirmed that it was run by someone old; no woman has been named Loretta since, like, 1947.) Said shop was for necessities, not heart-patterned bralettes with words like "spanky beast" printed on them, like my friends had. (OK, they didn't say "spanky beast," but they had, like, kissy-marks and "XOXO," which is pretty gross for a child to wear on her boobs.) But . . . no fun bras for me. No. We were at LORETTA'S SUPER SERIOUS INTIMATE MOTHAFUCKING NO FUN ZONE, and playtime was over!

While my friends with A-cups got to prance around in their adorable underthings, I was busy being fastened into triple back hooks and padded shoulder straps that I can only assume were meant for a work mule pulling an apple cart. I was a teenager, so my chest stayed up on its own, but guess what? These bras weren't made with youth or sexuality in mind, and these parachute harnesses weren't meant to be seen by a man, ever. These were bras meant to be worn by your squatty widowed grandma from the old country as she washed turnips in a bucket.

But there the fifteen-year-old me stood, at an age when I wanted to speak to my mother less than I ever have before or since, let alone stand there mute while she and some sixty-five-year-old Russian saleswoman manually scooped each of my breasts into its personal tit hammock as I attempted to pretend an outside party wasn't touching my private parts. "See, it should make you feel supported and secure." But . . . it was a bra, not a financial plan! I did not feel secure!

As a big-boobed woman, button-up shirts are also a long-standing issue that make clothes-shopping excruciating.

When your chest is big, sometimes you just feel . . . BIG. Naked it looks fine, but any attempt to shroud your chest with even the slightest fold of extra material just leaves you feeling like a pregnant linebacker. Even in a "minimizer bra"—yes, boys, there are bras designed with the sole purpose of making women's boobs look smaller—I always felt like I was wearing shoulder pads on my tits.

In my early twenties, with money of my own, to spend on any garbage I pleased, I sought refuge at Frederick's of Hollywood, a store for . . . hookers. Hookers and women who once did some light hooking but are now married to men who still need them to look like legit hookers. The bras are for show, made for huge fake boobs with straps made of something tenuous like one strand of Nerds Rope. Did I need a red sateen bra with flokati cups and little devil's pitchfork appliques sewn onto the straps? No. But compared to the oatmeal-colored straightjacket I'd been accustomed to, it was the most beautiful thing in the world.

Now let's discuss another body part that makes it difficult for many women to feel remotely comfortable setting foot in a mainstream clothing store: thighs. OK, this is the last time I will mention them, for real. Anyone who follows my comedy (and has, uh, read this book up to here) knows I don't like mine but I accept them, sort of. I firmly believe a lack of sinewy thigh encasing a long femur has stopped me from reaching every one of my goals. OK, maybe just when it comes to fashion.

Pick up any women's magazine when summer rolls around, and you're sure to find a horrific chart purporting to tell you what sort of bathing suit best fits your body type. Without fail, the model they'll use to represent the "curvy" body will be 5′9″ and 120 pounds, sporting a modest one-piece. This provides ample fodder for your Girl Logic to either embrace one-pieces for the rest of your life—"Hey, if it works on her, it'll totally fly on me even though I weigh approximately seventy-five more pounds and find running on a beach while laughing impossible"—or it leaves you thinking, "That is *not* what I look like in a swimsuit. The world is dark and empty. I'm wearing shorts in the pool. And the shower. And the bathtub. Forever."

So many shows, movies, and magazines would have you believe the key to success is a makeover. Feeling down? Makeover. Not living up to the aesthetic standards of your best friend? Makeover! Just murdered two people and the cops have your picture? Makeover! Does it ever occur to the magazine editors that some of us don't fantasize about a makeover? Some of us think we're perfectly fine as is. Revolutionary concept, right? Doesn't matter because the rest of society thinks it's their job to knock at your door insisting you start hating yourself a little more.

This happened to me in the mid-2000s. Back when Myspace was still a thing, I got an unsolicited message from a producer on *The Tyra Banks Show*. It was 11 a.m. on a Monday, and I was at my crappy temp job when I received the surprising offer. I'll never forget the wording: "We want to give you a makeover! You're cute, but you're not, like, a BOMBSHELL."

Nope, I wasn't, but . . . I don't know . . . fuck you? I was twenty-three and supporting myself with a shitty office job. I didn't *need* to be a bombshell. I wasn't upset that this producer didn't see me as hot; I was upset that he thought it was OK to tell me that.

Plus, no way would they give me the kind of makeover I would actually *want*. No way would I be getting blonde hair extensions, a spray tan, a push-up bra, and a white tank top. (I don't care what the standard is, I think '90s-era Pam Anderson is the hottest woman to ever walk the planet.) Makeover shows are created to make women like other women *more*. It's always "chestnut lowlights," a "fun" blazer, a chunky necklace, and a kitten heel. But . . . let's think about this. Why no spray tan and white tank top? Why no miniskirt or five-inch heels? Why is it trashy to show off certain parts of your body? Because men might be attracted to you and you might flirt or even—gasp— *have sex* with them? America's bizarre puritanical values are neatly illustrated through our makeover shows, where both women and men line up to take a crack at how we look and what we're doing "wrong."

And the rest of the world doesn't play by American standards of beauty, just in case you've never been issued a passport. Go to any Latin country or Europe and it's all hanging out. Naked kids everywhere, the elderly in speedos, men, women, children; flesh is everywhere. Good, bad, or flabby, no one cares. Everyone's fuckin' and everyone's cool about it.

Boyfriend jeans are another fashion fallacy that runs deep. But the fantasy element of these mythical jeans—denim that is beloved by every women's magazine around the globe but by no one else—might have your Girl Logic convincing you to buy into the following oh-so-romantic narrative:

You just slept with your boyfriend, and, after a lazy afternoon of sex and sharing ("We talked about his parents' divorce, and it got *deep*. We also realized we both LOVED Season 2 of *Fargo,* and that Season 1 was good, but nowhere near as good!"), you realize you're starving from all that mutually beneficial lovemaking. So you decide to head to the corner café and cuddle publicly. Maybe you'll wear a chunky sweater that miraculously doesn't make you feel like a sweaty llama. Maybe one side of the sweater will casually fall off your shoulder and a few tendrils of hair will haphazardly flip to one side, like Kristen Stewart in, well, everything she does. God I love her hair. Maybe you'll drink a seventeen-dollar coffee and not have to take a Jurassic shit right afterward. Maybe you'll sensually apply lip balm and not get your hair or scone crumbs caught in it like five seconds later. Anything could happen on this crisp fall day!

As you're getting ready for all that cozy coffee-shop loveliness, you casually throw on a pair of the BF's worn-in blue jeans, and because your hips are so slender and your legs so long, they hang off you like moss from an oversexed willow tree! You stroll casually to Le Cafe, passing outdoor patrons: "Oops, did I just cut open your cheek with my razor-sharp hip bone? So sorry!"

Your Girl Logic remembers seeing images like this in movies and ads for European coffee, so it instantly dumps you into

that fabulous fantasy landscape where you're the effortless in-
genue. Maybe you even trip while holding the coffee, you sexy
klutz from the intro! The reality, though, is far less glamorous.
Why would you ever need to don a man's ill-fitting pants? Did
you bleed through yours? Pee yourself? Oh my God, did you
crap your thong? Let's be frank: his pants look bizarre on you,
like it's 1995 and you're trying to look gangster but your mom
won't buy you baggy jeans so you're trying on your Dad's Orvis
khakis with a woven belt.

Now let's talk shoes! All women are supposed to love white
wine, gossip, and our financially and physically crippling shoe
collections, right? But no one tells you which shoes actually
look good with which outfits. Part of the problem is that most
shopping websites don't show models' feet. Like, once I bought
a knit Kenzo bodysuit with cut-out shapes all over it. It was hot.
I paired it with leather pants and . . . oh my God, what shoes?!
On the Kenzo website, they didn't show the model's feet!
SWINDLERS! Is it because they don't want to promote another
brand? Maybe. Or maybe it's because they're sitting in their
Paris atelier, scratching their heads, like, "Fuck, I don't know
what goes with this weird top either. Ah well, c'est la vie."

This leads me to believe that short of selling you the bodysuit and the lifestyle associated with the bodysuit, designers
have no idea how you're supposed to *actually wear* the bodysuit. They just want you to be a legless torso flopping about
snorting glitter with a severe cheekbone.

Then there is the mystery of the tunic, an item that is impossible to be worn the way fashion intends it to be worn. "It's

a tunic!!" has become the mantra for every salesgirl who is afraid to tell her customer that she is too heavy to wear said garment as a dress, so instead they instruct her to "pair it with leggings."

If someone tells you to pair it with leggings, that secretly means you shouldn't be wearing it. Leggings go with T-shirts and sweatshirts; they're not to be taken seriously. That's why they come in fun patterns like laser-eyed kittens and pink camouflage. (What is pink camouflage for, hiding from Valentine's Day?) Sorry, but I doubt designers are creating haute couture with the intention that, once it goes to market, "ze customer will just pair it wiz leggings." Average-sized women, having no official manual for, well, pretty much anything, are left to our own devices to figure out all this fashion shit on our own. So we started wearing leggings with Uggs, and men hated us for it. Deep down, I think they hated that we were comfortable.

At least we have our Girl Logic to help guide us, at least some of the time. Because while GL can be our worst enemy when it comes to fashion, it can also be an asset, encouraging us to experiment and think outside the box of what everyone keeps insisting you should wear. Like when your GL tells you to hold onto those clunky combat boots you bought your freshman year of high school because YOU NEVER KNOW. Or when your GL makes you buy that minidress that you felt ridiculous in at first, but now your boyfriend can't stop fawning over it. Of course, GL might occasionally nudge you into a pair of ill-conceived crotchless coral panties (because you want to look like you're ready to fuck in a cabana!), but if you're lucky, it might also send you home with a new denim jacket: the one infinitely cool clothing item that regular women and insipid fashion magazines can agree on.

My main advice when it comes to clothes and GL is to know and accept your body. Heed your Girl Logic when it's screaming at you to try something new and fun (um, provided it costs less than $500), but don't let your GL override what you know from experience will work for your body type. For instance, if you have short, stocky legs, don't let that works-on-commission shoe salesman—or your own well-meaning but overexcited GL—convince you that today is the one and only magical day that ankle straps *won't* make your legs look thick. If you have big hips, don't give straight-leg white jeans the opportunity to ruin your day. If you want to wear clothes that aren't in line with what you *know* looks good on you, you have three options. Get a good tailor, buy a brand that's expensive enough that there's a solid chance it'll be cut well enough to look good anyway, or, when all else fails, hold back your tears and go do ten sit-ups in the dressing room. Then go home. You probably already have something at home in your closet that will make you feel great, anyway.

My Handy List of Clothing Items
That Are Simply Never OK

Embroidered Jeans. As a traveling comedian, I'm horrified to report that people are still encrusting the curvatures of their butts with diamonds and circumscribing the borders of their jeans in thick white thread, like a murder victim's chalk-corpse outline. Did someone commit a homicide in your butthole? Then lose the white stitching. No one thinks the diamonds are real, and no one thinks you're a better Christian because you have crosses sewn on your ass. A bedazzled fleur-de-lis? You're not French, your last name is Sanchez. You're a mother, or, worse, a FATHER, and you want other citizens to take you seriously? These pants have to stop if we are to grow as a society. Trump wants to build a wall? Build a wall around the True Religion outlet.

Shirts That Say, "I'm a Mermaid," "I'm Really a Mermaid," "I'd Rather Be a Mermaid," "Yo Soy Mermaid," or "Je Suis Mermaid." Look, you're a grown woman, and that level of escapism isn't whimsical; it's irresponsible. You wanna check out of society, wear broomstick skirts, make beaded jewelry, and live in rural Oregon? Fine. At least you're still paying taxes. But when grown women say they want to be mermaids, it means that the world has been so hard on them that they've decided the best way to live is to project to the world at large that you want to be an imaginary fuck-toy for a horny sailor. And that scares me.

Bathing Suits with Hardware on Them. I think this one falls under the category of "Ludicrous Things Women Are Expected to Wear Without Making a Peep of Complaint." Like how Claire Underwood in *House of Cards* wears four-inch stilettos all day with tight pencil skirts on fifteen-hour flights and never untucks her goddamn shirt!? COME ON, CLAIRE! LET THAT SNOOCH'N'POOCH BREATHE! My point is that this trend where we decided bathing suits need to resemble Achaean battle wear is just, like, fashion at its most useless. Here is some basic science: hardware on a bathing suit is generally made from some type of metal. Metal conducts heat. Hot metal burns skin. Burned skin hurts and swells up and you will end up looking like you pledged a black fraternity. So I suggest you opt out of the heavy metal.

A Mule. This shoe is ugly, makes you look like you have a hoof, and they named it "mule," which is an ugly animal. I just hate it. You know what's sexy that a mule covers? Toes. You know what's not sexy that a mule *exposes*? Your calloused crackly heel. This shoe has everything backward.

2.5

Guy Logic: A Primer

Girl Logic forces women to consider the past and present, and how both inform the future, before making key decisions. What separates this type of thinking from the way men think is that women apply GL to every decision, even pedantic ones, like choosing frozen yogurt toppings. Men just don't sweat the small stuff as much, possibly because men aren't held to the same exacting social standards: men can be overweight, bald, loud, brash, and blunt and still be loved. When's the last time a man was dubbed the "office slut" and it was a bad thing? Or the last time a guy gained a little weight and the tabloids called him "pregnant"? That would be hilarious, actually.

The contrast between male and female decision making is most obvious in social situations, especially sexual ones. Of course there are men who meet a woman and immediately re-act with trepidation because of some crazy girl they slept with years ago, so they buy the current girl a drink while asking themselves, "If I bang her, do I want to deal with the potential emotional fallout in the morning?" But most aren't thinking that far ahead. They are, however, weighing the variables in the present. Variables like "How many more drinks until she wants to have sex with me?" "How many more drinks until she's so drunk that I *can't* have sex with her?" And, in some desperate cases, "How many more drinks until *I* will want to have sex with her?"

As men get older, they start playing the long game. Sometimes they even arrive at the conclusion that sex just isn't worth it if they're too exhausted, either physically or emotionally. Don't forget, there is a societal pressure on men to go out and pick up women; it's what guys are supposed to do, right? So when they see an opportunity to get laid, more often than not they'll go for it. Can't tell you the amount of times some forty-something male friend will confide, "This twenty-year-old I'm dating is running me into the ground." And I say, yeah, grandpa, keep up or chill out. Or, here's a novel idea: try dating someone who saw *Billy Madison* in theaters; it's not like women turn into the Crypt Keeper after thirty.

The thing to note about men is that, while not being as communicative as women, they are definitely clearer about their intentions, if you're paying attention. When a guy likes a girl, he shows up. He calls back, he makes plans, he isn't "just so slammed lately." The sooner young women grasp that, the less heartache and headache they'll have. There is no "he's just been so busy with work" when a guy wants to see you . . . or fuck you.

Clearly men are more action oriented than thought or feeling oriented. My theory is that this dynamic dates all the way back to prehistoric days. Men would bring back a dead animal (that women had to cook) as a way of taking care of you, or as a sign of affection; then eventually their offerings evolved to smaller gifts (which men brought because women couldn't buy their own, since we didn't really have jobs until the past two hundred years or so). These days, with women being totally self-sufficient, the most overt way a man can show you he's interested is simply by giving his time. And no, spending 12 a.m. to 6 a.m. with you doesn't count.

Guy Logic, in social settings with women, usually consists only of the question, "Will this get me laid?" Will buying this girl a drink and listening to her talk about how much she loves her niece and nephew get her to sleep with me? Will helping this girl move make her want to have sex with me? No earth-shattering secret there. And, yes, men are capable of being friends with women as long as he isn't attracted to her, or vice versa. Basically, you can be friends but only if one of you is cool with knowing the other one isn't into you. And there is the version where both of you just aren't attracted to each other, which is ideal. (Until you're single for a really long time and you start thinking, "Actually, Blake's kind of cute in that boy who looks like a hot lesbian kind of way.")

Men are also less high maintenance than women, as we all know. You can change plans, cancel, or shift things around, and they don't give a fuck. (Obviously everyone has a bullshit limit, I'm just saying that men *tend* to go with the flow.) Girls care. We care too much. If you tell me a time to be somewhere, or that you'll be there, or that you love me, I hold you to it. I once called a Lyft thinking a friend was already at the bar, and it was only when I was arriving at the bar that she called to tell me she was still home. I had to take a knee, because I knew I'd either drive to her house and strangle her with my bare hands or throw my iPhone out of a moving vehicle. And, guys? I did not want to buy a new phone.

3

Oh Boy, It's a Guys' Girl

Touching on what we just discussed, men are . . . different. This isn't a bad thing, per se, it's just true. They generally avoid overthinking, ruminating, or overanalyzing (three of women's favorite pastimes). They pursue what they want, or what they *think* they want, in a straight line without pausing to consider the questions that trip women up, like, "Will it make me look greedy if I ask for more money? Will he stop calling me if I express any semblance of interest? If I light this firecracker on my butt, will it ruin my chances of bearing children?"

Men who are not blessed with GL strike now and think later. Sure, women do that occasionally, too; bad judgment is universal. But, when it comes to basic instincts, women are simply more thoughtful, and Girl Logic has a big hand in that.

Another significant factor: men just don't have to worry about the same cultural standards that send our GL into a tailspin. They get to have more fun than we do, and they get to do it on their terms. A lot of what women do for fun in the modern age is stuff men got to do first (fuck as a hobby, read, drink, skateboard, vote, etc.). Men have always been allowed to be loud, make beer bongs, eat garbage late-night food, pass out wearing Wolverine costumes—basically, to behave like animals. (Again, they can thank their lack of Girl Logic for all that nonsense; most women know that beer bongs are never a good idea after age twenty-five.) Women, by virtue of the fact that we are physically more vulnerable, haven't partaken in the same degree of fuckery. Remember the TV show *Jackass*, which was all about boys daring each other to do reckless, needlessly dangerous, self-maiming pranks? There are reasons girls didn't come up with that first: (1) because what those dudes were doing was stupid and painful; (2) women don't usually have the same desire to test their own mortality; (3) if you want to have a baby someday, you can't be taking cannonballs to the stomach for a living; and (4) most of their prank's hilarity lay in some dude getting hit in the balls, it's just not as funny when a woman gets hit in the crotch.

Even so, women like being able to partake in fuckery if they so choose. Women now have the freedom to pursue their own version of happiness and can enjoy typically "male" entertainment: watching sports, drinking our faces off, snowboarding, or scream metal. And for some women, being "one of the guys" is something of a privilege—it suggests that you share not only their interests but also their freedoms.

I have to confess, I've always been something of a Guys' Girl. It's not like I specifically set out to become one; it happened naturally as a result of various factors, including my family background, which I'll get into shortly. My career path also led me to inhabit Man-Land most of the time; the comedy scene is predominantly male, so you need a thick skin and a masculine sense of confidence to get by. And part of why I'm funny might be because, though I look girly, I have a somewhat masculine sensibility that I know how to use to my advantage. I may be a Guys' Girl, but I don't suppress my femaleness; my GL is still alive and kicking. My GL sometimes causes me to worry about offending people. I worry about how men might be interpreting my confidence, even as I'm rolling with the guys. The combination of confidence and Girl Logic in comedy is a tricky thing: you need confidence to do this job successfully, but in the past, men have disliked me for it. And then of course doing this job well *builds* confidence, which can make a comic even *more* successful, and around and around we go. It's a Catch-22 wrapped in a riddle that GL will take a long time to sort out.

Anyway, as a lifelong friend of guys, it bothers me that, when society hears the term Guys' Girl, people automatically assume the woman in question is a bitch who can't be trusted, or a not incredibly attractive girl who drinks too much Bud Light and isn't above mud wrestling in a backyard kiddie pool. In reality, there are several types of Guys' Girls—and none deserve the kind of resentment and societal mythology they sometimes get. Here are a few primary GG archetypes with, as always, several iterations of gray in between.

Guys' Girl Type A:
The Sports Fanatic

This is the girl who loves, loves, loves sports, and it's a legitimate love. She usually played a sport growing up, maybe had a sports fanatic for a father or a brother, or maybe she even played at the college level. (Even now, in my midthirties, I still have a girl crush on any woman who was All-State anything.) These are girls who don't just enjoy the game but actually have a working knowledge of plays, and scores, and strategies, and coaches' names, and who does what on each team. Look at Erin Andrews: there's no questioning that she has a genuine love for sports, and she's not out there trying to be cute (even though she is gorgeous). Eventually, this love of sports becomes less present in many women's lives—I mean, you can really only rep SUPER hard for UConn basketball for, like, four months a year, then you gotta give it a rest. Same goes for Red Sox fans who have Red Sox—themed weddings. Man, that's gross.

Guys' Girl Type B:
The Other Kind of Sports Fanatic

This girl is typically just a fan of, well, whoever is hot. She's into sports because she thinks guys are into sports, and she uses her knowledge to manipulate her way into their hearts. She has Lakers jerseys that are actually dresses, and Cowboys jerseys that are pink and cinched at the waist. She loves to start fake arguments with guys at bars: "What are you *talking* about? Trestman is a pussy and their offense is shit." She wants guys to think, "Wow, a hot chick who loves sports and has a dirty mouth! DREAM." This type of Guys' Girl is simply mimicking male behavior in hopes of attracting a man, which, to be honest, does work. She knows just enough to get into guys' inner circles, which puts her at an advantage because she's usually the only girl, and thus gets all the attention. Well played.

Guys' Girl Type C:
The Drink Mule

Most of us are drinkers, but THE DRINK MULE is a type of Guys' Girl who tends to fade away with time. You can't be this girl after you've hit your thirties because you will either get alcohol bloat or die. Everyone knew that one girl in college who could pound drinks for hours with the guys. She was cute, but she didn't turn heads. She's the first one to drunkenly throw herself down a Slip 'N Slide or jump in the pool with all her clothes on, even if they're cashmere and her phone is in her pocket.

She's a guy favorite because she's a "good time," and she doesn't cry when she's drunk, like the rest of us. (One time on Halloween I got so drunk that I couldn't read, and for some reason that made me so sad that I had to literally be handed off between my friends Adam and Mark, who had no idea what to do with me. Eventually I stopped crying and convinced them that they should leave me at the bar, where I texted an ex at the other end of the city to come make out with me. I waited for more than three minutes, which in drunk time is an eternity, before jumping into an Uber and passing out at home. The ex was less than thrilled he'd driven from Malibu to Koreatown to discover me nowhere to be found, but, oh well. I'm sassy! Happy Halloween!) BUT it's impossible to sustain this life in a graceful way.

Guys' Girl Type D: The Hot Chick Dudes Claim Is "Like a Sister" but You Know They Secretly Jerk Off to Her Instagram Pictures

These are the *hot* Guys' Girls. This is more of a subset because the only reason this girl usually hangs around the guys is because the guys want to have sex with her (which, unfortunately, has a major impact on female self-esteem), and this makes her feel good about herself. There is often some sort of weird, unspoken competition going among her dude-crew about who can be the better friend to her. They know, like a shark smelling blood, that at some point she will be emotionally vulnerable; she'll need a strong trapezius to cry on. So they stick around. And she sticks around because, hey, they're trying sooooooo uncomfortably, embarrassingly hard. Maybe she even buys it! P.S. If her name is Kelsey, I guarantee they're all trying to fuck her. There are no ugly Kelseys.

Guys' Girl Type E:
The Stoner

This girl always has weed. Hence, she's ALWAYS DOWN to chill and eat, and watch a movie and eat, and drive around and eat, and walk in the park and eat, and go to the mall and eat. . . . Point is, she loves to hang. And eat. And watch *Faces of Death* until three in the morning. Guys dig this because there is no hassle. She often ends up ski instructing on a mountain or makes a hard life left turn and now has three kids and lives in rural Colorado, with her whole family in Teva sandals.

Guys' Girl Type F:
The Funny Girl

Being able to tap into what men think is funny is a winning strategy. Humor can win over a grumpy dude, a hot dude, or a nerdy dude, and it makes men feel at ease. By the same token, we all know that men with a stunning sense of humor tend to attract women who are way out of their league in the looks department—women dig nothing more than a deeply funny man (having money doesn't hurt, either). But when it comes to funny women, sure, men appreciate your scathing wit and dick jokes, but that doesn't necessarily make them want to sleep with you. Which is fine—the friend zone isn't always a bad place to be.

Do Guys' Girls have a different kind of Girl Logic than other women? Not necessarily. But we may have learned to adopt certain elements of men's ego-driven single-mindedness because, well, we want some of that power, too. On some level we've embraced the idea that if we could only act and think more like guys—move through life like a bull-headed plow and override our always-questioning Girl Logic—we might be rewarded like one of them. For years and years, decisions, laws, and social standards were all decided by white men in a board room, a bar, or a strip club, and if you could tolerate men drinking, smoking, and treating women like garbage, then you, too, could be tolerated in their work environments: "Let's have the board meeting at a strip club!" "Awesome, sir, I love other women's private parts and watching married men get lap dances. Great strategy to fix the Cranston account."

Traditionally speaking, the common perception of a Guys' Girl is a woman who's into "man stuff" like sports, drinking, murder, mass quantities of meat, and deep-fried fart jokes. Men were the first people who got to do anything exciting like sports, hunting, filmmaking, painting, and talking openly about taking a shit, so for a long time *everything* was a guy thing (except, maybe, sewing and child rearing). Hence, when I was growing up, being a girl involved in a "guy thing" always seemed cooler. Being a woman participating in a male-dominated activity meant one thing: you were "good enough" to run with the guys. Being as skilled and ballsy as the guys lent a girl a subtle air of superiority.

I became a Guys' Girl partly because I wanted to feel superior, and partly by default. Growing up, I was never part of a group of girls. Maybe I didn't fit in as a result of *other girls'* GL:

"If I don't hang out with the most popular girls, then I won't be popular, and if I'm not popular I won't meet any boys." I wasn't necessarily considered dorky or cool, though; I was just . . . there. I was never the first invited to a birthday party and I was never the friend people saved a seat for. The weird memory-scar of never feeling *quiiiiiite* good enough for the girls around me has played out in different ways, one of which is my desire to relate to women through stand-up. Part of why my comedy is so girl-centric is because I get what it's like to feel left out; my shows are my way of inviting everyone to sit with me.

If Girl Logic is a thought process that takes the past into account as a way to shape and inform the future, my GL has done its best to repeatedly warn me that women are going to, well, dislike me. I try to ignore that voice and be kind to other women anyway because the close girlfriends I do have, I really love. Like my best friend since I was three, Michelle. We're both often misunderstood, both challenged by men (she was often smarter than guys, or maybe her delivery needed work, who knows), and we both grew up with an insatiable curiosity about life beyond the Dallas county line.

We bought fake IDs together, snuck into bars together, threw parties, and colluded to cover it up when Michelle dented her car (because she was and continues to be the worst driver in the world; you can't deny it now Michelle, it's in print!). We even had jobs together. One time, to make money, we had the grand idea to drive up and down the Dallas Tollway, go through the toll and take all the money from the coin return that no one ever bothered to claim. Problem with that idea was that we had to pay to go through the toll in the first place. At the end of the day? We lost about eight dollars. She was the math genius; she should have seen that coming.

Michelle is the friend I throw my arm around and say "my boy's wicked smaaht," then I like to lick her face to annoy her. It's what sisters do. Michelle went to Tufts, the London School of Economics, and has a master's degree in something important that has nothing to do with comedy. After years of working for the World Bank, the Inter-American Development Bank, consulting for the OECD in Paris, and more, she settled with her now-wife, Grace, in Austin. She's hiked glaciers, hitchhiked across Australia, and learned three languages. All without stopping once to question what people thought of her. To say that I'm proud of her is an understatement.

Jodi is another close girlfriend. She's ten years older than me (I'm sorry, you are!) and was the first woman who befriended me in comedy. Before I was anyone in the industry, Jodi was my friend. I remember watching the Joan Rivers documentary *A Piece of Work,* and there was this tearful interview Joan gave about a toxic manager. She eventually cut him out of her life but admitted that, in doing so, she was basically losing the connection to an entire part of her past that only he remembered. For me, Jodi is that lifeline (she's not toxic, though). Without her I lose an entire chunk of my twenties, the men I dated, the shitty shows she and I did, the horrible comics who started with us, she's the only one I have left to cross-reference these experiences with. Loyalty is hard to come by in Los Angeles, and so is compassion. Jodi is talented and beautiful, and has always been there for me. She's the kind of friend where, when something horrible happens, I can't wait to tell her so we can make fun of it together. She makes the pain of working in comedy funny.

Andriana, another close girlfriend, is someone I met during a Semester at Sea, a life-changing experience I'll talk about more later. She was . . . tan. With bleached stripes in her brown hair. She had a lower back tattoo in Chinese and was from LA, obviously. But she was fucking smart. She went to Berkeley, which I thought was so cool—she looked like the girl who would steal your boyfriend, but she secretly had morals and a major in political philosophy. She had the kind of scathing observational skills that made me say, "Oh my God, I can't believe you are saying this out loud because I'm thinking it quietly." And I think part of me was just so pumped that a girl who looked so cool and was so popular wanted to hang out with me so much. The day we met, she walked up to me and was like, "You're that funny girl." I was like, "You're that hot girl" (I thought that, but didn't say it), and a friendship was born of drunk trips and ghosting on parties to go off and eat together on our own. She is the friend who will take a vacation with you even if you have to work the whole time, and on more than one occasion she has pretended to be my publicist. She is also my girliest friend: the one I call to ask if an outfit works. She would never call me for fashion advice, and if I ever tried to give it to her, I would imagine she would casually sniff, "No, my outfit works, but thanks." She knows what's in style, which restaurants have hot chefs—she is my *Harper's Bazaar* and *Zagat* guide in heels, and she's not above going as a "sexy nurse" for Halloween, even in her thirties, because she doesn't give a fuck.

The common denominator among my women friends is consistency. They show up, they care, they don't judge, and they all knew me before I became who I am today. Being alone with any of these women makes me feel like, together, we are enough.

Growing up, I didn't always feel that way. In fact, it wasn't until I started writing this book that I realized how lonely my childhood was. Even from a young age, I never believed I should be treated poorly just because I wasn't winning popularity contests. I remember changing to a new school in third grade and wanting to be friends with this popular girl named Shannon. Shannon had an inhaler and carried it in a purse, so you knew she was mature. I asked her if I could play with her, and her response was, "Fine, but only on Tuesdays and Thursdays." I told her to go fuck herself. Kidding; I didn't say that, but I also did not take her up on her pathetic offer. I didn't find it painful back then, but most people don't realize the collective pain of all those tiny social paper cuts until they're adults. So many of my contemporaries have faced down darker demons; what right did I have to complain, or be sad? I wasn't raped, or raised in poverty, or kicked out of the house at fourteen. My trials and tribulations—being raised by a single mom, bouncing from school to school to school, never quite feeling like I'd found my place—seemed to pale in comparison, so I tucked them away.

I also used them as motivation. That feeling, as an adult, of hoping people know and care that I exist manifested itself in small ways. For instance, when I signed autographs, I wrote "ILIZA" in a big blocky print, instead of an illegible cursive scribble. That way, people would see my name and know that someone had asked for my signature, that I'd been there, that I mattered. I still do it to this day.

Anyway, on the "uninvited" front: When I was sixteen, I went on a group trip to Spain. I was the only kid from Dallas (all the other ones were from New York and Los Angeles). Parents, don't send your kids abroad with kids from either of these cities. They have money, an appetite for drugs and booze, and, at sixteen, are worse than your average twenty-one-year-old. Jesus Christ—one of the girls brought a whole bag of dildos. At sixteen, all I wanted was a T-shirt from Abercrombie, and this girl had a BAG OF DILDOS. Who sold them to her?

Our whole program of about twenty-five kids headed into Madrid one afternoon. After congregating at a cafe for lunch, my roommate Amanda and the other "cool" kids all plopped down at a table together, squeezing me out and leaving me standing there awkwardly alone. Amanda offered, "Oh, you can just go sit over there; we can hang after lunch!" pointing to a table of dorks that none of us knew. My Girl Logic began screaming, "But . . . if you don't hang out with the cool *girls*, you can't meet the cool *guys*!!!" (Hey, at sixteen, nothing mattered more to me than meeting the cool boys, obviously.)

Not wanting to show that their flippant casting me aside had cut me so deeply, I disappeared into the street. I was fucking starving, and pissed, and hurt. My Girl Logic was *still* screaming at me, "If you aren't friends with these bad girls or cool guys, you will spend your summer alone! You'll go back to Texas miserable and ostracized, with no new friends and knowing that absolutely *no one* knows you're cool!"

I think being rejected by women from a young age built up my desire to connect with women as I grew older. As an adult, I get it. There have been plenty of women who've been drawn to me as friends that I just . . . wasn't into. Nice enough, cool enough, but we didn't click. But when you're a kid with limited social opportunities and fragile-ish self-esteem, feeling rejected doesn't just sting; it makes you question your entire being, your purpose in life. And, growing up, every year there was at least one or two girls I desperately wanted to be friends with who wanted nothing to do with me. So I started hanging out with the guys instead. What was my alternative—befriend local wildlife and talk to trees, or sit with the dorks who were actually on this trip to, like, learn? Come on.

Of course, hanging out almost exclusively with dudes creates its own special variety of petty dramas, especially when you're young. You're bound to develop some crushes on them, and the lines between friendship and romance can easily start to blur. Growing up in Texas I knew I wasn't pretty enough to be with the hot jock, the class clown, or the quiet bad boy type. (Do those exist anymore? We all know how Christian Slater in *Heathers* turned out.) Taking a cue from my divorced parents, I couldn't be with someone *just like me*. Back then that meant no class clowns, and today it means no comedians.

I mean, don't get me wrong; I *love* comedians. Sometimes I watch comedy and get turned on. Not so much by the comedian, mind you, but by their act. If I could fuck their act—if I could ball up all the brilliance and timing and make it into a sentient being to be intimate with—I gladly would. Some of my girlfriends have suggested that because I'm "strong and outspoken," I need a strong man: a professional athlete or a celebrity. And I remind them that most starting quarterbacks aren't into wandering around Hollywood in their pajamas looking for cheap Korean foot spas. Plus, I take issue with the phrase "strong woman." What does that even mean? Am I giving birth, roadside, fixing a flat tire while I hold the car up with one finger? Am I pulling a Mack Truck with my teeth? I think being a strong woman has just come to mean that you make money, have your shit together, and refuse to apologize for either of those things. I doubt Elon Musk would look at my single-car garage and income tax statement and think, "Nah, too strong."

Anyway, it's a universal principle that two things that are exactly the same tend to repel each other. That's why you can't put two positive sides of a magnet together. My parents are a great example of that. My mother is outgoing, smart, and pretty; she, too, is "one of the guys." Even though she was a Guys' Girl like me, my mother certainly wasn't immune to the ups and downs of a brain powered by the blessing/curse of Girl Logic. I saw it play out in her life every day. "If I don't go to work, then I can't provide for my children, but if I miss out on something at home, then I'm a bad mother. If I date too much, then I'm setting a bad example, but if I don't date at all, then I'm a lonely single mom of two." In the end, she was able to do it all, as most mothers are forced to do. And because she was attractive, her GL was always whispering, "Remember, other women might find you threatening, so don't be too nice to their husbands. But also make sure to always look put together because you never know who's out there."

Maybe seeing her experiences unfold helped push me toward identifying more closely with the men in any given room than with the women. My dad is the funniest person I know and he's teeming with jokes, charisma, and . . . I guess he's good-looking for a dad? (I mean, he's no Robert Herjavec. And no, I'm not worried about my dad feeling insulted after reading this. He's not going to call and say, "What, you don't think your dad is attractive? But this is a brand-new fleece vest!") Point is, my parents were drawn to each other because they saw in the other what they loved about themselves. But eventually that mutual admiration became a competition, and that competition became a divorce, which became little Iliza being forced to see a therapist to make sure she was OK when all she really wanted was to collect crystals and watch *Ren and Stimpy*.

So, yeah, my parents divorced when I was seven and my brother was five. At the time, I was actually pretty OK with it. I wanted them to be happy! Sounds weird, but I truly don't recall being upset. I'm sure I had my moments, but it just sort of . . . passed. I never thought about it as I got older because, well, every couple eventually seems to get divorced. What was so special about my parents? To harp on their divorce like it was some sort of albatross felt trite. As trite as referencing an albatross.

It wasn't until I was an adult that a therapist informed me I hadn't fully "processed" everything that had happened back then. We lived in Dallas, and my father had moved out of our house and into an apartment, like dads do when they leave. (The best part about divorce is that your dad's house is always more fun. There you can eat junk your mom won't buy, like Jell-O pudding cups and Fresca, watch TV longer, and lie about homework because your dad has no idea what subjects you are studying anyway.) Then he got married and moved away to Stamford, Connecticut, for work. So by the time I was nine or so, my father was living 1,500 miles away with his new wife, Barbara. I know kids are supposed to hate their step-moms, but Barbara was a nice woman who was madly in love with my father. And she really tried to be cool with my brother and me.

But my dad was gone, which meant it was just my newly single mom raising me and my brother, Ben. I felt like my friends were safely ensconced in their happy, complete little family units while we were the one weird family that had gone through an amputation. I felt this vague sense of em-barrassment for most of my childhood, like we were some-how less than, like we were being judged. And we were, for sure. I remember my mom saying she overheard other moms whispering about her when she dropped my brother off for soccer practice: "She's divorced. Her husband moved away," like she was some freak with three heads (and two kids to top it off).

I was never embarrassed by my mother, of course. I was mainly sheepish about the fact that my father *wasn't* there. So, to compensate, I started seeking out male approval through jokes. It was always important to me to make my friends' fathers laugh; I already had my mom's love, so this was my way of connecting, of feeling loved and "guy approved." I like to think learning to decipher what makes a grown man crack up—to tap into an audience that was my utter opposite—helped my comedy improve and mature. It also primed me for becoming a Guys' Girl.

My mom did the best she could to serve as both mother and father. She lost a bunch of friends after the divorce; no one wants a pretty, newly single third wheel hanging around, and I saw the way women dropped her after the split. Fewer invites, less inclusion. When my parents were married, my friend Katy and her family always invited us over for Thanksgiving dinner. Then, when my parents split, we stopped getting invited. One year Katy's mom invited my mother and me, but it was very clear that the invitation was only for dessert, not for the actual meal. Ugh. Reminded me of Shannon's "Fine, but only on Tuesdays and Thursdays."

Once, my mom and I were watching my brother's soccer game. Soccer wasn't so much something my brother enjoyed as much as it was something my mom wanted him to be involved in so he could be around other boys. My mom sat on the metal bleachers, the only single mom in the crowd. She was there to support him, of course, and who knows what work obligations she'd had to skip or errands to postpone to be there for him that day.

It had rained earlier that day. As she was getting up, she slipped on the bleacher. She tumbled a few seats down and skinned her leg on the metal edge of the bench, slicing open her left shin. My mom sat down, blood running, bone exposed, wincing and crying. I was ten, and all I remember was being *angry* that she was crying. I remembered knowing that my feeling of anger wasn't fair to her but being mentally unable to override my anger with concern, so I eked out a simulation of sympathy: "Mom, are you OK?" Of course she wasn't OK. It wasn't OK that she fell, that she was hurt, or that she was drawing even more attention to our shitty little fatherless family. And it wasn't OK that no one cared. One woman finally came over to help her clean up her shin, but . . . that was it. None of the other moms around us said anything, did anything, or showed a modicum of compassion. Was it because they didn't know her? Because she was Jewish? Because she was the sole single mom in the crowd? Because she was attractive? Who knows? Years later, my mother told me that after the incident, my brother had innocently asked, "But why didn't any of the *dads* help you?" Somehow my mother's solitariness had made her radioactive.

On the brighter side, my mother would be thrilled to tell you all about that one time she dated a dashing Jewish man (I say that because anyone Jewish reading this will understand what a rare superlative "dashing" is for us) named Richard, eventually bringing him to temple services with us. As she sauntered into the synagogue with him, she heard a woman whisper, "If she can get that, I'm getting a divorce, too."

When I was about twelve and my brother ten, my father moved back to Texas with Barbara. He wanted to be near us because my brother "needed his father." Seems simple enough, right? My brother Ben ended up moving in with them, about a five-minute car ride away. After that, Ben wasn't a huge part of my day-to-day life. He eventually moved out of the house to go to military school for a year and, when he came home, just sort of made his own path, not a traditional one—then again, some people aren't cut out for normal rules. By the time I went off to college, I don't think Ben was living in the house with my father anymore. Though we lived our separate lives, we treasure the few years we did spend together under one roof (fighting), and we talk every now and then. He lives on a farm in Northern California and is very very happy. I'm happy for him. He's also very good with kids and animals and is a good-looking dude, ladies, in case you're ever in the area.

Even though my dad, stepmom, and brother lived just a few blocks away, I never felt super comfortable in their house. He and Barbara went on to have two other kids, and, as their family grew, I accepted that my father had bigger responsibilities now. There just . . . wasn't as much room for me. Sure, I was welcomed whenever and was always included in holidays, but my home was with my mother.

But, the older I got, the more the divide seemed to intensify between my father and me. I was also a teenager by then, so I wanted nothing to do with my half siblings—what teenager wants to hang with little kids? What were we, a family band? I vividly remember being about nineteen and storming out of a Maggiano's because their kids were too loud. I'd brought my college boyfriend to dinner and the combination of secretly sort of hating him *and* the kids intermittently screaming with no parental repercussion was like a powder keg. Where did I go after I stormed out? I think I just sat on a bench outside while Sinatra played. Whatever, I was making a statement. I should also say that their kids grew up to be great. We aren't close. In fact, Brad, my half brother, and I had our first real conversation in my dad's kitchen about a year ago. We were both shocked by how much we liked each other. My half sister Emily is a year younger than Brad and she's a singer and lives in LA. I don't see her much because the idea of getting drunk with a minor gives me major anxiety, but she's a talented singer with a great sense of style. I'm thirty-four and I low-key stalk her Instagram and think, "Oh, thaaaat's how you wear loafers, got it."

When I was about fourteen, my mom married my stepdad, Randy. He was nothing like us. Randy was Waspy, went to Harvard Business School, and wore polo shirts that had yacht club names embroidered on them. From the day I met him, he was nothing but supportive; I lucked out in the stepdad department. He stepped right in and gave my mom a break. They both worked, but now life was easier. More normal. I loved my father, and Randy never tried to compete with that; he did, however, fill that space at the dinner table that had been empty for so long. Randy was, and continues to be, a warm presence in my life. He is not funny, but he doesn't have to be. We started saying "I love you" a few years ago, and it feels right. My relationship with Randy showed me that men who aren't related to you can still be capable of loving you.

When I met Randy, he was divorced with three kids of his own, the youngest being about my age. It was just like my previous situation with my dad—he lived across the country from his kids. He loved them, and I was able to see exactly what sacrifices he would have made for them. He was always there to listen and help with my school; he even took me to look at colleges. He never made me feel like I was some lost nobody with divorced parents. He wasn't Jewish. He wasn't Christian really either but he just, ya know, definitely wasn't Jewish. No Jew has that many houndstooth blazers. And when he and my mom got married, we got to have a Christmas dinner. GOD IT FELT GOOD. (Most Jews secretly want to do Christmas stuff; Christians have better PR than we do.)

Throughout my high school years, my mom and stepdad attended my plays, games, and events. My dad came to as many as he could, but I doubt he ever felt fully included in his daughter's world, especially when it was my stepfather who had truly helped create that world. It kind of got divided up in a way that my dad took care of my brother and my mom took care of me. Basically, if you went to high school with me, you probably didn't meet my father . . . who lived just a few short blocks away.

I never questioned it at the time, but to this day "family" is a fragmented idea to me. Still, I'm grateful for my four parents. They've pushed me to pursue my dreams and have all been supportive in their own way. My stepmom never judges. She was an actress when she was younger, and, when I was about eight, she took me to an audition for the box cover of a tetherball set for a sports company. I booked the gig. It's the only professional modeling I've ever done. Granted, the image they chose was of me blocking the ball from my face, so I look like I'm seizing but so what? Work is work.

My father loves comedy and his sense of humor is something I've always cherished. He gets comedy, better than anyone I've ever met and, as an adult, whatever mending our relationship needed, it happened through us bonding over comedy. When I was sixteen, he took me to see Ellen DeGeneres at the Majestic Theater in Dallas. It was me, my dad, and a room of lesbians. It was my first stand-up show ever! Seeing her shaped what I expect from women in comedy; Ellen was funny for a person, not just "for a girl," and I carried that standard into my own career. About a year ago, I got to play the Majestic Theater, and my Dad was there that night. It was one of those full-circle moments that you have to stop and let steep in for a minute.

My mom enabled me and emboldened me to become the woman I am, and, at times, has pushed me to be more of the woman I *should* be (or maybe just the woman she wants me to be). When I call her from the road, when I'm bleary and teary, when I have the flu and am trudging through O'Hare at 6 a.m., when I tell her I have to leave Thanksgiving early for work, when I say she can visit but I can't see her because I'll be on set, she always understands. She's never done the "Jewish mother" thing and bugged me about getting married or having kids. She just lets me be me and tolerates that I'll always be a little sloppy and bad at cleaning. Her answer is always, "The situation will crystalize."

My family history definitely played a part in me becoming a Guys' Girl. Being "friends" with my stepfather while feeling I had to play a more adult role around my actual father helped me learn how to be myself around men and helped me realize that there wasn't any one way I had to behave for men to appreciate me. Inheriting my father's sense of humor and my mother's boldness, coupled with the opportunities my stepfather afforded me, I never felt like I wasn't allowed to contribute equally when I spoke to men.

For example, I remember once, when I was eighteen, my parents had a friend over. Mike Malone was one of the top guys at The Richards Group, Texas's largest advertising agency. I came out of my room to say hi, and, when Mr. Malone asked where I was going that night, I told him "Bingo." (Michelle and I were hipsters ahead of our time, apparently, in our ironically-but-it's-also-kind-of-fun-to-play-Bingo-with-old-people phase.) Mr. Malone replied, "You know, my mother died while playing Bingo." I shot back, "Guess her number was up?"

Was it risky to make a joke about a man's dead mom? Sure, but he put it out there. Thankfully everyone laughed, my stepdad thought it was hilarious, and so did Mr. Malone, who, right then and there, offered me a summer internship. Point is, my fragmented family, with both of my fathers helped me learn that I was on par with them; to see myself that way and to expect to be treated that way, too.

But my parents' divorce has always served as my personal cautionary tale. Knowing I'm just like my mother *and* my father, I didn't want history to repeat itself. I didn't want to be with someone knowing it could end up in divorce because of something preventable. So all my life, I've looked for men who *aren't* like me. Men who are funny but not screaming to be the center of attention. Men who are centered; not all over the place, like I am. Men with a quiet strength and confidence.

My somewhat male-like ego, my childhood practice of trying to make my friends' dads laugh, and my aforementioned difficulty getting accepted into groups of girls all led to my having a lot of guy friends. I'm not going to lie and tell you they were all the hot guys you were secretly praying would ask you to prom. But, every year, I would have a new guy friend who liked me solely because I made them laugh, and that was good enough for me. Guys might read this and think, "Um, duh Iliza, they just wanted to hook up," and who knows, maybe some of them did. But I have plenty of good male friends who have been my friends and colleagues, feature acts and confidants, for years. I think after years and years of high-quality, nonsexual friendship, it's safe to say they might be cool with us just being friends. Give men some credit.

Also, I will say that being a Guys' Girl *did* help me in one significant area of my life—and without it, I might never have cemented my passion for stand-up.

As I said earlier, when I was twenty, I participated in a college program called Semester at Sea. It's basically a cruise ship that, for a semester, houses about six hundred kids from various colleges. Together, you and your peers sail around the world, taking classes on the boat and stopping in different countries to get drunk . . . I mean, learn. "Ek aur biyara chahiye!" That's "one more beer, please," in Hindi.

On the boat there were three guys who hailed from Arizona State. These were stunning men—blond hair, blue eyes, jawlines that could cut glass. Every girl on the ship wanted them. I did, too, but I wasn't terribly familiar with casual sex, and I had zero desire to compete. I made them laugh, which to me, is right up there with getting off. At an open-mic night, I got onstage and made some jokes about the ship—the food, the students, the staff, the hookups. The next night, everyone was hanging out when the hot Arizona guys walked right up to me and demanded, "Hey! We're bored. Can you make us laugh?"

As an adult, working comedian, if someone said that to me today, I'd roll my eyes and retort, "Sure, pay me." But at twenty, with no act and seven extra pounds of wine fat, doing every Will Ferrell impression I knew was the closest I would ever get to making out with them. And with that, I was in. I was the funny girl. And funny is FOREVAAAHHHHHHH.

After that night, I was often invited into their room so we could all watch *SNL* DVDs. Whenever I'd hang out with the hotties, I noticed girl after girl trickle into their rooms, trying to gain entry under the guise of having lost something. "Hey guys, did I leave something in here when I was studying earlier? Did I leave a . . . book?" They'd ask if they'd left sweatshirts, brushes, pens, hard drives, bras, or tampons, anything to get back in. It was ridiculous. But the next week I went onstage and imitated those girls with their high-pitched voices. (FYI, that's where my "girl voice," a sort of cartoonish amalgamation of girlish intention and inflection, comes from. When men imitate women, they always make us sound like drag queens, with overpronounced *s*'s and a Valley Girl–ish "over it" sound. To me, girls sound brighter, more high pitched, like a chorus of sped-up chipmunks.)

Anyway, that was my first attempt at girl humor, at letting women know I could understand and recognize them while also, well, poking fun at them. That humor about Girl Logic—and Guys' Girls, and girls' girls, and all the weird and personal confusion and communication in between—has been the basis of my act ever since. Of course, as I mentioned earlier on, my girl-focused humor wasn't always warm and fuzzy in the beginning; as I've grown older and wiser, my comedy has evolved into something that appreciates women's GL-fueled nuances and quirks without bashing them for it. Let's face it, if I thought I was hot enough to sleep with them, I for sure would have pretended to forget something in their room.

Being a Guys' Girl is great in your twenties—you can go to bars with men and feel safe. Plus, your pals usually have a hot friend or two, so you can make a move or try to set your girlfriend up. Once in a while you also forge a bond with men that actually transcends sex. Recently, I took one of my best friends, Mark, on the road with me. I had to change in a hotel room for a gig, so we went upstairs, and he watched TV while I changed in the bathroom. It occurred to me that the only time men and women are in a hotel room together platonically is when they've haphazardly botched a kidnapping or bank robbery and have to form a strategy. Unless of course you have a history of being a Guys' Girl.

I can definitely tell you, though, that being a Guys' Girl isn't all it's cracked up to be, especially as you get older. In your thirties, do you really want to be the only girl surrounded by drunk sweaty dudes at a Super Bowl party talking about all the chicks they banged but didn't care about? Do you want to be the girl your guy friends only opt to hang out with when they're between relationships? Do you want to be bloated from two decades of chugging beer and find yourself with absolutely zero women to relate to because while you were out high-fiving bros and eating hot wings, the other girls were forming lifelong bonds with each other thanks to ClassPass?

I spent my twenties competing in a mostly male environment, working alone on the road. I had missed baby showers, weddings, and kids' birthday parties, and now, rounding my thirties, I found myself coming up short in the female-friends department. I still had my best childhood girlfriend, Michelle, who lived in Texas, and my best friend in Los Angeles, Jodi, but I wasn't drowning in brunch buddies. I needed a core group. *All* women need other women in their lives. I was finally seeing women for what they were: gorgeous treasure troves of shared experiences, knowledge, and understanding. I was getting lonely onstage, talking about the girl experience but not living enough of it.

When I was about twenty-nine, I remember getting dressed for an important meeting, and I froze because I had no clue what to wear. I FaceTimed a girlfriend in New York to consult, but no answer. I scrolled through my phone: Mark, Steve, Marc, Josh, Mark K., Chris, Mark P., James. One thing was clear: I knew too many guys named Mark. Another thing? I didn't have enough women friends! All my life I had been a Guys' Girl by default, and now I found myself with very few women to talk to about real grown-woman shit like:

- Why having a sugar daddy makes sense and doesn't necessarily make you a bad person.

- What it's like to have vaginal tearing.

- Being hopelessly in love with a man who will never love you back.

- How to treat hemorrhoids.

- Where did this hair come from?

- Why can't you stop pooping when you're on your period?

- What it's like to meet the man of your dreams but still be in love with an ex you despise.

- Why it's unfair that we got educations and took care of ourselves, and now there's absolutely no quality men left to date.

- Why am I starting to hate everyone?

- Seriously, why is there a hair on my nipple!?

- Is it bad to fuck a guy who rides a skateboard?

The fact is, Girl Logic starts to shift gears as you grow into an actual adult. In your thirties you become more selfish, in a good way. You begin to put yourself first, whether it's being upfront about wanting a relationship, craving more alone time, or needing to sleep all day. You gain a sage new perspective, and you can look at twenty-three-year-olds freezing outside a club in heels and minidresses and think, "God, I remember doing that, and I'm so glad I'm not doing it now." Also, if you don't know the owner of the club by the time you hit your thirties, then you're doing something wrong.

In your thirties most relationships take a serious turn (even if it's, uh, a wrong turn), and all your guy friends pair off and start getting married—even the gross ones you wrote off as incapable of holding down a legit relationship. All of a sudden your best guy friend is dating a graphic designer who isn't all that bad looking, and they're flying to meet her family in the Bay Area over the holidays, leaving you alone on your couch on Christmas Eve, thinking, "How is this happening?" Yup, one by one, all your closest guy friends start to move on and pair off.

For all these reasons I've grown out of my all-dudes-all-the-time days. Over the past few years, I've made a concerted effort to make more girlfriends. These days, I want someone to get a pedicure with. A friend who will watch me try on five black shirts in a row and give me her uncensored opinion about the minute differences of each one. A friend to bemoan about the awkwardness of sex—"OMG, WHY was he moving his hips in a circle?" Someone to listen while I insist that I'm "totally over Derek" as I proceed to gush about him for thirty minutes straight.

This is part of why women are important to each other—because we all share Girl Logic, and a beautiful arrhythmic heart, and topsy-turvy emotional brains that tell us we need to have it all. We should be drowning in guy friends *and* girlfriends, *and* have a fulfilling career, *and* a hot boyfriend, and ALL THE THINGS. But in reality? Most of the time we're just pining to talk to another female who gets us . . . and who also hates everything.

4

Sex: A Comprehensive Guide— JK, but I Did Write a Lot

When it comes to sex and dating, Girl Logic can get a little messier—and more messed up—than in other areas of life. Sex is particularly fraught for us because Girl Logic causes us to constantly question our bodies, our impulses, and what we really, truly want.

A lot of times, I really just want to sleep. Sometimes I want to make out. Occasionally I will have moments like "OH MY GOD I JUST WANNA FUCK," but then I spend so much energy examining the what-ifs that it leaves me exhausted and I end up aborting the mission. That's all Girl Logic, the detailed surveying of every emotion as it passes through. But next time you're in the moment, ask yourself: Do you actually want to FUCK, or is that just because everything you see on TV suggests sex should be aggressive and primal instead of slow and awkward, the way it is in real life? You're supposed to want to wear Agent Provocateur lingerie and be "made love to" on a kitchen counter, but in reality marble is cold, that underwear is expensive, and orgasms can happen on a bed with your sweat-shirt on. (I have them all the time, both alone and with my fiancé.)

Part of the problem is that what we *think* we want—especially when we're young—and what we *actually* want are not the same. GL is the voice of insecurity when we're in our twenties, that battle of "I'm drunk and I want to touch someone but what if I do and he rebuffs me? What if I do and he sleeps over and then never calls or texts me again? What if I get hurt? Can I just be sassy and not care?" GL causes us to think we want to act like dudes and casually sleep around, but, oops, that whole oxytocin thing kicks in like gas on a fire, spurring crying-in-the-shower and spontaneous-new-haircut behavior.

A lie our Girl Logic likes to tell us when we're younger is that if we just fuck him, things will go more smoothly and he'll like us more. The thing your GL didn't tell you is that no one has ever said, "He wasn't into me, then he broke down and had sex with me and fell in love with me." Nope, it's usually, "He wasn't into me, we fucked, and he still wasn't into me . . . but I was even more into him." OR, "He wasn't into me, we had sex, and he was terrible and now I'm not into him." OR, "He wasn't into me, we fucked, I got pregnant, now he's a father to my child and he barely tolerates me." OR, "He wasn't into me, we fucked, I got pregnant, and he quickly found a new girlfriend, dumped me, and now I'm an angry single mom and the villain in all his life drama."

Wanna know why dating is so hard for women, though? Because we aren't men. We don't think like them, we don't date like them, and we don't communicate like them. Fortunately, by the time you're older and more experienced (and are properly exhausted after years of worrying about what you look like, what others think), you eventually realize what really matters and what doesn't; you start caring less about what other people think. But that doesn't mean there aren't plenty of stumbling blocks for every woman, of any age, when it comes to sex.

If you find sex frustrating—no matter your age—you aren't alone, you aren't weird, and you aren't doing it wrong. Getting off is easier for guys, no secret there. The secret is that women don't get off, oftentimes, because sex is just more personal for us. After all, we're the ones hosting a stranger INSIDE our bodies. It takes tons of time and dedication to know what you want sexually, and it takes the right guy—maybe not the love of your life but the guy who will put some work in and actually *wants* you to get off. Point is, you won't know you aren't having good sex until you have good sex.

Good sex may be hard to come by, but women shouldn't be ashamed of their desires *or* their mistakes as they strive for it. Shitty sex and heartbreak are relatable; everyone's been there. And choosing to hook up with strangers does not make you bad, nasty, or "slutty." (Whatever, church ladies still use that word, right?) In fact, I encourage women to have as many partners as they want so they'll figure out what *they* like. But there's the rub (yeah, rub it good): when you're young, it's rare to know what you want sexually, and it's often in hindsight that you can see you might have slept with someone for the wrong reasons.

To find a partner who actually cares if you get off is a beautiful thing. Women are taught to consider their orgasm as a secondary priority, after the guy's. And sometimes, when ours is elusive, we just roll over and say, "Whatever, I'm fine." I'm thirtysomething and I still do that! "You got off? Great, get me a towel and bring me a Snapple. I wanna watch *House Hunters.*"

Now plenty of women will read that and think, "Oh hell no, I am *not* fine until I get mine!" But I doubt you were always so empowered. When you're younger, your Girl Logic leads you to believe that you're pretty much solely there to be sexy for the guy.

Of course you want to enjoy sex, too, if you can manage it—but you're also aware that if your own orgasm is not incredibly likely to happen, you don't want to bore him by making him go down on you, right? Or you're afraid of what he'll think of your vagina, or you don't want to take too long?

You can't blame young women for being self-conscious about their bodies. Dear God—if you take a minute to bask in the sophomoric treasure trove that is Instagram, you'll see all kinds of garbage women-shaming posts like, "If her pussy be lookin like a tired roast beef sandwich. . . . " And then all the douchebag idiot followers adorn the comments section with "crying laughing" emojis, like any of them would turn down any kind of vagina, EVER.

Male genitalia has become synonymous with fun, strength, and power. But how is it we're meant to ignore people's lack of decency, grammar, and overall comprehension of labia, but we're supposed to be chill about how 100 percent disgusting ball sacks are? Not only that, but we're supposed to accept the use of "balls" in everyday conversation (balls to the wall, balls out, suck my balls, have huge balls), the implication being that these nasty hanging alien brains are somehow synonymous with a fun, bold party time? BALLS TO THE WALL! Fucking gross, dudes. And so easy to make fun of. (I admit I've been known to occasionally scream, "SUCK MY DICK!" But no one gets called a pussy unless he's a sad coward.)

Anyway, the younger you are, the more likely you are to let adolescent commentary seep into your brain and allow absolute idiots who have probably never seen a woman naked to make you feel insecure about your own body. And while it's trying to ultimately steer you toward good shit, Girl Logic is not always your friend here. Women's sexuality is such a vulnerable thing, even something as simple as one insensitive comment can scar you for life. When I was in my early twenties, I had a boyfriend who loved me . . . but told me my vagina was too big. His penis was average and so was my vagina, but he made this diagnosis and substantiated it with "it's not your fault, it's probably from playing sports." Apparently playing JV outfield can really come back to haunt you. The insanity and inaccuracy of his statement didn't matter. The idea stuck with me, and his insecurity about his penis gave way to my insecurity about my normal vagina.

Honestly, enjoying sex is a bipartisan effort. I have been in serious relationships where I was rarely getting off but the guy claimed to adore me. You have a responsibility to stand up for yourself sexually and let the dude know: "You gotta spend twenty minutes down there. Bring a flashlight, pack a lunch." You have to know that your pleasure (I hate that word) is just as important, if not more so, than his. Because when the only sex you have is bad, you start convincing yourself it's good sex. And then you keep spreading around terrible sexual experiences until someone takes the time to teach you better. I remember almost freaking out when, at thirty-two, I had sex with a thirty-six-year-old man whose kisses were so wet I needed a spit bucket. I had to take a break halfway through and go to the bathroom so I could wring out my face and hair, and abstain from murdering him while naked. All I could think was, "Who's the bitch who let him get away with kissing like this?"

I'm a comedian, so of course I *have to* talk about sex. It's the lowest common denominator for relating to people because everyone has a relationship to sex, even if they're not having it. Laughing about sex comes easy; it's almost innate. But being crass about sex feels sophomoric; doesn't sitting around chortling about lube mishaps instantly remind you of depressing, Bud Light–drenched college parties where the girls all peal about how rough they like it and the guys brag about their impressive five inches of fury? I don't even know if I got off during college. But if you asked me back then, I would have told you I loved sex—whatever sex I thought I was having.

Speaking of which, I remember telling my freshman-year boyfriend, Alex, that I wanted to have "rapper sex."

"What are you talking about?" he laughed, rolling down the window of his black Pontiac in front of his frat house. The problem was that I *didn't know* what I was talking about. I was eighteen, and I knew almost nothing about anything, despite the fact that I was managing to have tons of sex with Alex (who, in retrospect, had a really small penis. Sorry, dude, you're a psychopath and your dick was subpar. MAN, THAT FELT GOOD!).

I'm Jewish, though, which means I've been listening to hip hop since I was eleven, and rappers make sex sound like an ice cream sundae and a Carnival Cruise rolled into one. In my fantasies, there was just enough masculine heat to keep things interesting, as well as champagne fizzing on naked bodies, and massage oil, and hot tubs, and everyone was getting off all over the place without the need for a vibrator or real-time fantasizing about someone else, like that kid in my psychology class . . . who I *wasn't* having sex with but we were like, kissing and stuff, all while rationalizing that I wasn't cheating on Alex, the psycho. God, I was awesome. I mean, dumb. I was dumb.

This was all bound to remain my little fantasy, though, because massage oil is nasty in the bedroom AND because no one in college has a clue what actual sex is *actually like*. Women just don't get off at the slightest touch of a man—the second he grabs your boob or puts his hand on your thigh. Nope. For most women, having an orgasm is going to take a little (meaning: approximately thirty minutes, give or take) time and effort and a lot of check-ins: "Are you bored? Is it gross? Tell me if you're tired." That effort is obviously worth it—don't give up, my young friends. And for the love of God, please don't fake it! FAKING AN ORGASM IS LIKE CHEATING ON A TEST. Sure, in the moment you get an A and look good, but if you don't actually possess the knowledge you're being tested on, you'll just fail miserably when a bigger, more comprehensive exam comes along.

And don't think orgasm-faking isn't GL-related; it totally is. GL can go into hyperdrive during sex, telling you to do more, feel more, look sexier, come faster—all in a passive-aggressive attempt to make the dude think you're irresistible enough to fall in love with, thereby ultimately fulfilling your GL-fueled fantasy of perfect forever love and validation. The thing is, faking orgasms is lying to yourself as much as it's lying to him. Not to mention, next time the dude's gonna think, "Wow, she really liked it when I called her 'baby boo' and clacked my teeth against hers while we were making out! I'll do it again. And again. And again." He never learns what you like, and it's an orgasmless vicious cycle that ends with . . . wait, it doesn't end, it's a cycle. What a nightmare.

Something that tends to change for women moving from their twenties into their thirties, though, is our definition of "promiscuity." From eighteen to twenty-two, you're probably in college, and, although you are meeting new people, you are still in an enclosed environment and moving in a group. Groups have gossip. Groups have history. Your business is everyone's business. You are all navigating your new social playground together, and you haven't shed the habit of gossiping intimately about each other's lives. Girls get called sluts because too many people know too many stories about them. Guys get called "players" for the same reason. But the older you get, the more you take charge of your own life, and the fewer opportunities people have to judge you because they *don't know* what you do on the weekends. They're busy with their own lives.

So, with any luck, by your thirties you've outgrown this groupthink mentality of labeling people for their sexual habits. You just might be having sex more and caring less. Plus, you've spent the past decade figuring things out, dating and fucking and being judged and learning. Your Girl Logic has naturally evolved and changed with you, and now it's less concerned with your friends' sexual pastimes—or fulfilling some idiot's fantasy in bed ("oh my God, please wear a red lace nightie")—and more concerned with making your own dreams into a reality (whether that's fucking a quarterback, falling in love again, dating a twenty-two-year-old, testing every single one of America's top-selling vibrators, or getting thyself to a nunnery).

Your twenties are also the decade of every man you date demanding to know how many people you've slept with. I lied every time anyone asked me that—not because anything was "wrong" with my number, but because almost any number you give will be seen as bad. If I had a monogamous boyfriend every year since becoming an "adult" at age eighteen, if you asked me my number at twenty-seven, that'd be ten guys. All he would hear when I told him that would be, "Ten dicks that are bigger and better than yours that I think about ALL THE TIME! I LOVE DICKS! I'M ONLY WITH YOU TILL I CAN GET ALL THOSE DICKS BACK IN ME! Ten! Ten! Ten!"

Point is, in my twenties, my Girl Logic was still a little bitch a lot of the time, worrying what men thought of me and how to spin the truth so they wouldn't feel insecure. I didn't know enough about sexual empowerment to say, "The number is five—get over it, you're just lucky to be with me." (The number was seven, but it's a universal rule that there are some guys you don't count. You passed out after one thrust, Drew, so I count you as half a point.)

Now that I've navigated through a few adult-ish relationships, I can't imagine a man asking me for my sex number. I can't imagine caring what *his* number is, and I can't imagine sitting here counting up my own tally. I travel a lot and my free time is precious, so when I'm free, if I'm not staring at my phone habitually refreshing Instagram, I just want to hang out with my close friends. None of whom give a fuck who I fuck, because we're old now and we just wanna laugh and/or scream at how bad (or, hopefully, good!) the sex was. We aren't interested in making each other feel bad about having it in the first place.

In any case, though, sex is a lot easier to come by nowadays thanks to the advent of online dating. But why has no one seemed to figure out that the people you "heart" on dating apps are usually nothing more than a reflection of your passing momentary mood? (And on that note, why do these apps always use a heart to indicate interest? They should use a clickable GIF of a girl making the eyeroll-y "fine, I guess I'll go" face.) Sometimes I'll have too much coffee and get all frisky and overcaffeinated and be like, "Neck tattoos?! HE COULD BE THE ONE!" Then, when I'm feeling irritated and picky after a bad date, I shuffle through the same catalogue of losers, only this time like, "Only Jews with blue eyes and large hands who live in Del Mar!"

After I've passed the initial heart-GIF-click-a-thon and made it to the far-off point of actually sleeping with someone, I admit: I'll mentally check out if you don't hold my attention during sex. I will check out so hard I could finish a *New York Times* crossword puzzle (Sunday edition, thanks) while we're fucking. In fact, I only remember having amazing sex a handful of times in my life. To this day, the best sex of my adult life was with a total stranger I met while I was abroad for a few weeks doing shows. So, in the spirit of sharing, I will tell you this ONE fun sex story. Even though this particular relationship didn't lead to true love or anything, it illustrates a time when my Girl Logic had my back.

I had never been a fan of one-night stands, and had never had sex with a stranger (OK, maybe just one other time) and I figured, "Hey, I'm in this foreign country for a few weeks, I have my days free and a flat, might be nice to have a companion for a bit." So I went out a-hunting—that is, I went dancing with some friends I had made that night at a bar. It was the first time in my life that I'd left the house with the *goal* of finding a hot stranger and making him my temporary paramour. Simultaneously trepidatious and exhilarated about what I might find in a European market (bad teeth? fun accent? most likely anti-Semitic?), I set out. And there he was, in the middle of the dance floor, blond swooping hair and an Aryan smile so strong that it would make Hitler say, "See? This is what I was talking about!" He was in skinny jeans and a Polo shirt with a giant stripe across it. He was gorgeous and obviously not American.

He told me he was Swedish. The hookup gods were smiling upon me that night because he spoke English quite well and had great teeth. We walked back to my flat, intermittently making out. I was reticent to share with him what I did for a living, because it isn't sexy. Having to explain that I'm the kind of famous where some people care and others don't is a weird thing that does not remotely qualify as foreplay. He said he watched a lot of American TV. I assured him he had never seen me. Also, him being Swedish, who knows what season of *Law and Order* they were on over there. We got back to my place, and I soon uncovered something I wasn't prepared for but should have been: he was uncircumcised. Being American and Jewish, I had never encountered this before. My ignorant side came right out with red, white, and blue sparklers and a Bud: "What do I do with that? It looks like a Russian grandma wrapped in a shawl."

He replied, "Why would I be circumcised? I'm not Jewish. Most of the world's men aren't circumcised. I can't believe you've gone this long without knowing that."

What got me was his . . . maturity. I was thirty-two; he was twenty-seven and looking at me like the hideous American idiot I was acting like.

He had tapped into an insecurity of mine: the fear that I do not, in fact, know everything. He was right, of course. Still, meeting a new penis is one thing, meeting a new penis that doesn't look like any other penis you've ever met is a mental hurdle you have to clear quickly if you want the night to end well.

I needed a minute. I went to the bathroom and, of course, got my period. I sheepishly came back to the room and said, "Sorry, I can't do it; I just got my period." He didn't even blink. He ripped my underwear off and said, "What am I, in kindergarten? I don't give a fuck." (But he said it with an accent, so, like: *I down't geev a fahk.*)

And we were off to the races. It was a combination of his beauty, confidence, and his unwillingness to let my own mind get in the way. And we just fucked. And I never once, that night or in the subsequent week we spent together, thought for a second that he wasn't 100 percent into me. My GL was actually telling me to enjoy it: "You never allow yourself to just be casual and have fun. This one time, let yourself do something you genuinely want to do without judging yourself for it. If it doesn't work out, no big deal, because you're going into it wanting nothing more than to try. Also you don't even live on the same continent! Also he carries a messenger bag and wears a lot of Polo!"

But the thing was, I legitimately went into it wanting nothing more than to have fun for the time I was there, no strings attached. Which wasn't always the case for me—women often lie to themselves about this stuff, saying things like, "I just wanna see where this goes," when we know the guy is all wrong.

Some part of us even thinks, "What if he's the one?!" And those expectations, buried as they may be, end up hurting us in the end. Lucky for me, on this one night in this one particular year of my life, my GL was encouraging me to let go of all that preoccupation with the future and just have a good time.

The next morning, I rolled over, exhausted. He was watching something on his phone. I stared at him, still the epitome of pristine Swedish attractiveness, an epitome I was basing only on him since he was the only Swede I'd ever met.

He looked over and said, "Your last name is Shlesinger, isn't it?" I thought, "Oh God, something anti-Jew is about to come out of the mouth of this uncircumcised person from a country I don't even know enough about to make fun of." And he held up his phone to a YouTube clip of me hosting the dating show *Excused* and said, "This was my favorite show! I used to watch you all the time!" Then we FUUUUUUCCCKK-KKED TO CLIPS FROM MY SHOW. Kidding.

I'd like to thank him right now for being so arrogant in his pursuit of sex that night.

I'd also like to suggest, based on my own personal experience, that one thing *every girl* should try, even if just for the laughs, is to have phone sex with someone whose first language isn't English. That's right, the Swede and I kept in touch, and we ended up having fantastic phone sex. Not only would he narrate the naughty events he was imagining, but he would also tell me what he fantasized *my* reaction would be. So it wasn't merely, "I'm going to throw you on the bed and fuck you"—nope, it became, "You're going to walk into the hotel and I'm going to throw you on the bed, and you'll pro- test and say, 'Oh, but I've only just arrived, I haven't even had a chance to unpack my toiletries.'" HOT. (Update: We only saw each other during that one trip, but we say hi on WhatsApp every once in a while and talk politics, who we're dating, whatever. We're friends, and about as close as two people with nothing in common, nothing holding them to- gether, and an ocean between them can be. I'd also like to thank his parents for not circumcising him because the man I'm in love with now is also not circumcised and it made get- ting to know his wiener less awkward. Still looks like a cold Russian grandma in a shawl, though.)

In my twenties, I was almost always in relationships. My Girl Logic kept telling me that's what I was supposed to do, not sleep around, because if you are sleeping with someone, you should be dating them. Nowadays, having had a few one-night stands, and, recognizing the bizarreness they can bring, I see that my overly monogamous twenties might have been a mis- take. Or . . . not.

OK, ONE MORE SEX STORY. I'd met Jack on this "celeb- rity dating" app. He wasn't the celebrity, I was. Amazing, right? Having never done online dating before, I chose that outlet be- cause it seemed to offer something of a filter. I didn't need to date another actor or even a famous person, but you had to apply to this site and get, like, approved. Basically, I wanted to date someone similar enough to the point that I didn't end up on a date with my Uber driver. So I met this Jack, and he was cool and handsome. He even *called* me. LADIES, DID

YOU HEAR THAT?! My phone rang! I was like, "Wow, what the fuck is this old-fashioned move-maker doing!?"

I was playing in Denver, and I'd bought some pot; my plan was to do my show, come home, smoke alone, and draw with crayons later, so I deliberately put off the pot-smoking till after the call because no one likes weird weed talks. I also didn't want to think or talk about dying, which happens every time I smoke pot.

Anyway, after we talked, we texted for about a week before things got spicy. I was bored and somehow we started—dear God, I hate this word—"sexting." (I hate sounding like a fifteen-year-old or, worse, a mom trying to relate to her fifteen-year-old. "See, honey? I got a pink clip-in hair extension! We're best friends, let's take a SnapChat!")

But our sexting thing was pretty hot, and my radar was picking up on the fact that he had a huge . . . hog. Go for the quiet ones, ladies—they're always the ones who are packing the meat-heat. (But not too quiet—the super reclusive, socially rejected ones tend to shoot up public places. Then again, maybe if you *do* go for them, they'll get a little female attention, and they won't feel so goddamned TRIGGERED all the time. Maybe you, and you alone, can help prevent a mass murder!)

So one night he came over. I had been on set all day and still had on my camera makeup. That shit is designed to make you look flawless through a lens, but up close after ten hours, your face looks like the surface of an oatmeal cookie. It was midnight and I had to be up at 7 a.m., but . . . he came over. Supercharged sexual gratification guaranteed, right? My GL was telling me to go for it. ("Be bold! Fuck him! You hardly ever do this stuff, but you'll feel so good afterward, just like how men feel after they fuck! Like they just conquered something!")

We got AFTER IT . . . for five minutes. That's five minutes total, including taking off our clothes, getting in bed, having sex, and then inhaling the palpable air of disappointment afterward. It was boring, and *nothing* like what was promised in the brochure! He'd promised me not just an orgasm but fun! Adventure! Rapper sex! (He was white, but so?) Now the typical male response here might be, "Maybe you, Iliza, just weren't that good." Girls, if someone ever says that to you, then they've either *never* had sex or they've been so stunted by society's never-ending porn fixation that they think *women* are supposed to love all sex, no matter how bad. It's on guys to make it great. The girl shows up and gives him a soft, warm place to put his penis—that's hospitality! Anything beyond that is a bonus. You would have to lie there crying and motionless while staring at a picture of your ex-boyfriend for a man to be able to solely blame you for it being bad. You might not be the greatest at sex but I still think it's on the guy to do most of the work.

The truth was, the moment sex was over, I was motivated by one thing and one thing alone: sleep. Now it was 2:30 a.m., and I had little skin snowflakes all around my mouth from kissing, which apparently had exfoliated my makeup off. I went to the bathroom for approximately eight minutes to wash my face, and when I came back, the dude said, "You aren't talking to me." While I was indeed disappointed by the sex, my silence actually stemmed from the fact that I had been in another room under a running faucet for eight minutes.

Then he said, "You're treating me the way men treat women after sex," and I confess: I kinda loved that. So I told him, "I need to sleep—you're welcome to stay, but if you can't, no worries." ("No worries," a.k.a., the motto of every Australian youth adapted by modern American daters to illustrate that they are carefree when, in actuality, Americans aren't built like that. WE CARE. We just don't want to be seen as clingy, and so we beat you to the punch and act like we care *as little as possible*.)

He sat there puzzled, then opted to leave.

Of course, my Girl Logic seized that moment to begin whispering quietly, "Maybe I should stop him, I don't want to be rude, blah blah blah." But sleep was all I could think about, and I knew that every second he sat there debating what *he* wanted was one less second I had to sleep and fix my face for the next day, which was what *I* wanted.

That experience reminded me that, when it comes to sex and dating, taking a second to check in with yourself and ask, "What do I really, *really* want right now?" can be incredibly useful.

After that night, I decided I would never let that happen again. If someone starts texting me sexual things late at night, I won't just give in out of boredom and loneliness and ignore my exhaustion. I should have gone to bed and been fresh for the set the next day. This goes beyond feminism, it has to do with taking care of myself in the long *and* short term.

These days—as in the months before I met my current boyfriend—when a man I'm not in a relationship with says he wants to have sex with me, I first ask myself, "Will this benefit me? Will I get off? Is it going to be fun? Will it be more fun than sleeping?" Most likely not. If the only aftereffect is the *other person* feeling amazing, well, then I see no solid reason to do it. Then there are the guys you decide to sleep with despite your better judgment. No matter how much self-respect I dole out to myself, and no matter how long I hold out to have sex in a decent relationship, there are some men who are irresistible despite being just . . . Blazing. Hot. Garbage. Fires. You know the ones—they pursue you like crazy, then never call once you've expressed a whiff of interest. Or how about the ones who talk about commitment in this easy breezy bullshit way that women NEVER allow themselves to do, lest we be branded desperate psychos. I'm talking about the dudes who are on a third date, then all of a sudden they're dropping shit like, "Hope the kids get your sense of humor" or "Gin drinker huh? Well, you'll be a whiskey gal by the time we're married, har har har!" He might sound lighthearted, but believe you me, these kinds of comments are manipulation; he's playing with your emotions, and that's not cool. Your Girl Logic will kick into overdrive, picking up on that sniff of a future promise, thereby prompting you to overanalyze your own degree of interest. "OMG, *am* I into him? *Could* I be into him? He is making commitment-y sounds with his mouth, so maybe he's serious?! Could I fall in love with *him*? Is *he* in love with *me*? I knew I'd find a relationship man one of these days! Holy shit our kids ARE gonna be cute! I *will* be a whiskey gal!"

And yet, if you uttered any of those thoughts to a man, they'd be terrified. Didn't you know? The rule is that men *make the rules,* and women *navigate around them.*

On a semirelated note, dating can even get weird when you *don't* sleep with the guy. When I was twenty-three, I dated this man for a few weeks and never had sex with him. (For what it's worth, my general rule is that, when you first start seeing someone you're into, always put sex off one date longer than you'd like to. If he actually likes you, he won't mind. You will never regret waking up not having had sex, and it will always just make him more determined.)

In this case I moved slow, and he was thirty-six and so pumped to be dating someone my age that he was down to wait. I broke it off with him after I saw a professional e-mail he wrote that was so riddled with grammatical errors, it looked like it was penned by a gifted fourth grader. Another interesting thing? After I broke up with him, he got mad, and, to try to make me feel bad, he faked his own death. Yes, you read that right. He had friends instant-message me to tell me he'd died. As if I would be like, "Oh no, he died! Turns out I *did* love him—I see that now as I stare tragically at his poorly written obituary."

But hey, whatever sex-related bullshit we're dealing with at any given time, at least we have Girl Logic to help us navigate through the minefield that is modern romance. Because you know that expression "be your own best friend"? At the end of the day, your GL should—and can—be yours. You'll fight sometimes, and she'll drive you bananas with her incessant demands and critiques. But after emotionally terrorizing us when we're young, GL ultimately helps us sort through our personal values, figure out who we are, and pin down who we want to be with, in the bedroom and beyond. As a grown-up, I still occasionally get tripped up in matters of the heart (or, uh, matters of the dick). But all the crap my GL put me through in my twenties helped me pin down what I deserve and what I want—in bed and in relationships. It helped me realize, for once and for all, that no man is worth as much as my own self-respect. And my sleepy time.

5

Perfect Love, Perfect Life:
The Ultimate Girl Fantasy

Women's near-constant pursuit of perfection is the engine that drives Girl Logic. Especially when it comes to relationships. GL, wanting us to have all the things and be all the things—sometimes simultaneously—encourages us to build elaborate fantasies about our dream relationship and what we want from it. Which isn't a bad thing, of course; GL can help determine precisely what "perfect" means to us and cheer us on as we strive for it. The problem is when we start believing that our fantasies are imminently attainable and literally nothing else will do. (Sound familiar? Bridezillas are a good example: "I SAW A PICTURE OF A LIVING CRYSTAL DOVE ONCE AND I *NEED THAT* AT MY CEREMONY, OR MY MARRIAGE WILL MEAN NOTHING!")

Another pitfall: GL can encourage us to want a zillion things all at once. You want to dance barefoot in a downtown loft till 5 a.m., making out with a sexy Spanish model . . . but you also want to wake up fresh faced and "hit the gym" with a partner who genuinely worships and respects you. Girl Logic always reminds us to take stock of the past, for better or worse. You might have always dated bad boys before. Even though you know you don't want that in your current relationship, you can't help but miss it a little when you're strolling through a farmer's market with your new guy, who likes buying lavender in bulk. Even though we want our futures to be "perfect," it's hard to shed our old ideas of what we used to love and move into the unknown of what we might actually *need* to be happy.

Women cobble together fantasy notions about the "perfect man" from movies and novels. Then we find ourselves disappointed when said man shows up because he's 5′1″, eats with his hands, and wears a cinched-waist leather coat from Wilsons.

Then there's social media. We see all the beautiful women on Instagram with their doting spouses on their arm, the two smiling kids, the golden retriever named Bailey, and the barn-chic anniversary party she's throwing together between meal preps and running marathons. We see her, and our GL starts whispering that our current partner isn't enough. We start wanting what *she's* got. We start questioning the choices we've made and the things we truly want. We start feeling shitty about this happy but imperfect little life we've built, thinking maybe there's someone else out there who's better for us. Even if this is a person we're in love with!

Fantasies about what we *should* want are forever enshrined in our culture. Everyone knows fairy tales are garbage, yet they're the first stories we hear. Whatever happens, never fear: in the third act, a prince will save you. Take a closer look and those stories are filled with helpless women and idiotic inbred princes. In the end, Belle from *Beauty and the Beast* was so desperate to get away from Gaston, the hot French misogynist, that she was willing to fall in love with *a lion in a tailcoat.* She so wanted to be left alone to think and read, and she could only find a creature who appreciated that once she had left town, gotten herself locked in a castle, and fell in love with a giant feline that walked on its hind legs and wore a jacket! She was planning to fuck a giant housecat in a dinner jacket! That's where said story would have gone had that weird magical rose curse not been broken and he turned back into a human.

In these fairy tales, all the princesses experience an "all is lost" moment until someone saves her. Sleeping Beauty falls asleep, Snow White eats the apple and falls into a coma (She was in a fucking coma because a jealous witch poisoned her! Women have been fucked from the start!), Jasmine is for sure gonna get raped and murdered by Jaffar, the Little Mermaid will never get her voice back (she gave it up to be with a man) . . . and then! When it seems like all is lost, the prince shows up to rescue her.

You can't blame women for wanting to believe. Our Girl Logic is still hardwired to think, "If I do what society says, if I stay pretty and take care of myself and am independent but still vulnerable, then surely my own perfect White Knight will appear." They all came for the princesses, right? I can't help but think of that episode of *Sex and the City* when Charlotte exclaims, "I've been dating since I was fifteen, I'm exhausted! Where is he!?" If dating were merit based and the amount of effort and time you put in were directly proportional to what you eventually got from it, then life would be . . . fair. Sorry, kids.

The only reason we should strive for anything resembling "perfection" when it comes to finding a partner is so we can feel loved and supported, not so we can fulfill a childhood Disney fantasy, impress our friends, or freak out and cry, "I did the work, I put in the time, now where the fuck is my human reward?!" For some of us, the reality is that we'll spend our lives building an identity, going to the gym, and making our own money, seeking out happiness in the form of friends, travel, culture, and food. Then, in our thirties (or later), we'll wake up, look around, and say, "I'm the best possible version of myself! Universe, I'm finally ready for a partner!" Oops. Sorry, sister. He's already married, "super busy with work," or threatened by you because you floss *and* brush.

The deepest irony is that the fairytale princesses somehow maneuver a prince into saving them when they're at their *weakest*. When women in the twenty-first century realize we're ready for love, we're usually at our strongest, which sends certain lesser (but still desired and eligible) men running in the other direction. In real life, there is no saving. In real life, when you're lonely, disappointed, and burned out and you find yourself in an "all is lost" moment, you know what happens? Nothing. You cry a lit-tle, maybe watch *Chef's Table* on Netflix all day while eating a can of olives and cheap chocolate left over from Christmas. The next day you wake up, tired, and . . . you keep living. That is, if you didn't choke on an olive, alone in your house. Your best friend returns your text like five hours after you're done crying, and by then you don't feel like talking anymore. The only e-mail that comes in is a reminder from Allstate about your policy renewal. No one saves you; certainly no man. There's only . . . you. As Carrie points out in that *Sex and the City* episode: "Have you ever thought that maybe we're the White Knights, and *we're* the ones who have to save *ourselves*?"

And yet for most women, our Girl Logic still embraces the fantasy, and we measure ourselves against it. We love to collage lovely vignettes of perfect possibilities—that's why so many women are obsessed with vision boards and Pinterest. When I was a freshman in high school, this guy in my grade, Dan, was dating a girl named Mary who was a year older and just *so, so cool.* She had a nose ring as a tenth grader! I still remember standing next to them one day as she was hyperbolically pro-claiming she was "stressed out" and "losing it." She wailed, "Ugh, I'm a mess," and he cupped her face and said, "Hey, you're a lot of things, but you're not a mess." And she closed her eyes and laughed and he kissed her forehead, and, unbe-knownst to them, I was standing five feet away, watching the whole thing and having a moment.

For some reason I latched onto that sound bite. I don't know why; I'd had boys say cute things to me before. But that couple just seemed so . . . mature. She seemed so adult in her self-diagnosed hysteria, and he was so assertive, reassuring, and in control. I carried that snippet with me through high school, college, and into my twenties. I decided that one day my Perfect Guy would say that to me, and it would be SO, SO SPECIAL. Well, he finally did. Kind of. Except he didn't turn out to be my Perfect Guy.

I was thirty-one, and he was my boyfriend of a few months. We were inside a very well-lit Hollywood 7-Eleven and, in a chemically induced amorous fog, I decided to try to make that one high school memory happen in real life. Feigning being frazzled and tapping into my already natural wellspring of annoyance toward most things, I declared, "Oh my God, I'm SUCH a mess!" and he responded, "You're not a mess." He said it! He actually said it! Fairy tales do come true! Then, noticing I was holding three different bags of Mexican cookies, he noted, "You're just a monster." Then he tickled me and I got annoyed. I might have accidentally farted quietly. It was nothing like I had hoped for.

See? Nothing is perfect. Not even the "perfect" moments we dream up, like that one. If the universe can't even manage to create perfect moments, then how are women, in all of our mortal complexities, supposed to be perfect, look perfect, or have perfect relationships? The simple truth is, our obsession with perfection isn't just about what we expect from men—it's about what we expect of ourselves.

Everyone knows nearly every model in every ad campaign is photoshopped. But that doesn't stop us from secretly thinking *if only* we looked like them, then our lives would be perfect. The rational knowledge that those ads are fake—that in day-to-day life, no one looks like a model all the time—doesn't stop our Girl Logic from whispering, "Maybe I, too, can effortlessly wear a vintage football jersey and have it skim my privates while I flit around a Super Bowl party laughing, unspilled cocktail in hand."

All this model-worshipping nonsense has triggered an epidemic of body-image issues. Intellectually we know that whatever flaws we're obsessively harping on, chances are, males don't notice. Eight percent of men are colorblind, for God's sake! And though women may never truly appreciate this fact, our bodies aren't ugly. "Muffin tops," stretch marks, cellulite—it's all normal.

I'm going to admit this: I'm disappointed every time I look in a full-length mirror and don't see a model looking back at me. Somehow my time away from the mirror allowed me just enough momentum to concoct a new fantasy about what *might be there* later on. Then, when I look again and don't see mile-high legs and a perfectly symmetrical face, I'm shocked: "Huh! That's not what I expected." I also expect to always look as good as I feel. Which is impossible because I might *feel* fine about last night, but my face and under-eye circles tell a different story: Moscow mules, dry skin, and Party Goblins.

I'm also shocked when a man doesn't give me a second glance. Not because I think I'm a supermodel (we've already established the deal on that) but because movies have taught us that if you're the star of the film (a.k.a. your own life), then that perfect guy will notice you, no matter what. It's the reason single girls get dressed up to go to the grocery store. We all, deep down, like to think that our light shines so bright that some sexy, sweet stranger will see it through all the cracks in the surface and call us onstage at the One Direction concert. What? Not One Direction? That's not a band anymore? What's left, the Chainsmokers? Are the Wallflowers still touring? Never mind. We all like to think we're attractive enough that a cute guy will suddenly walk over and say something like, "Excuse me, I couldn't help but notice the bright, beaming glory of your soul shining through . . . ," and then you can be like, "Cool! Is that a Wilsons leather jacket?"

But part of us always fears our inner light is about to burn out. This can be blamed partly on biology. Women have a finite amount of time to have children, and many women happen to want them, or think they want them, or at least want to leave open the possibility of wanting them somewhere down the line. And why wouldn't they? Getting married and having kids is held up as the Ultimate Climax Perfecto Moment of Womanhood from pretty much the moment we're born! But the clock is ticking on these future children, which means we have less time to date and even less time to go through that murky period where you just give hand jobs and refuse to keep the lights on during sex. It feels like, after twenty-one, you have a week to figure out the narrative of your life, find a partner, and decide when and with whom you'll be making babies, if you choose to make them. Now, obviously I've exaggerated that time line, but this idea of a fertility shelf life creates a feeding frenzy as we get older and causes standards to drop ever lower in the dating department.

When our GL starts descending into panic mode, it tells us that if we don't act now, we might end up past our prime and "miss our window" on love or kids. GL whispers in our ear: "Just pick someone already; grab the next normal-looking carbon-based being who talks about wanting a family." But here's the fantasy I subscribe to: The window never truly closes on happiness. Even if your ideal life always included being a mom, that doesn't mean your life will become a meaningless void of despair if for some reason you don't end up having kids. Maybe you'll adopt. Maybe you'll foster. Maybe you'll become a tutor. Maybe you'll open an animal sanctuary, or babysit a lot, or realize you always hated children after all (oops). You can always find new paths to fulfillment. Easier said than done, I'm sure, but there can't just be one kind of happiness for everyone. And in those situations, even though I know GL is trying to push me toward what it thinks I need, I have to step back and calmly tell it to calm the fuck down and leave me alone. You can't force time, or fate, or whatever. Meditation can also be handy, if you're into that, from what I've heard. I don't know, I was busy.

In my twenties, I remember hearing thirty-five-year-old DINOSAURS talk about dating. They would jokingly say things like, "I just want him to have a job and know how to make a dinner reservation." And I would think, "Ew, how lame are those women?" Now, in my thirties, I'm saying the exact same thing. It isn't that my standards dropped, it's that my expectations are lower because I know through painfully lived experience that quality men get taken quickly. Because men don't have that godforsaken biological clock, endlessly ticking, louder and louder, "Tell Tale Heart"–style, there isn't always the same urgency to "make it work" with random women.

As a no-longer-young woman trying to find the right man, sometimes you need a real push-comes-to-shove moment in order to stand up for yourself and tap into the part of your Girl Logic that innately knows and wants what's best for you.

Here's my moment: I matched with someone on a dating app, and he asked me out. His profile on the app was . . . fine. He was Jewish and normal looking; you know, the kind of normal where if he'd had a stellar personality, then everything could have been incredible. So we went for a drink. I had refused to give him my number, justifying that if we could make a plan via the dating app and it worked out, then I would give this stranger my number.

I should have bailed when he walked in five minutes late and mildly sweaty from walking over from his office. Letting the woman know that you made the date as convenient for yourself as possible isn't exactly a turn-on, right? But hey, desperate times call for desperate dates!

We talked for about an hour. Things were going . . . well. Which, on the gradient scale of dating, translates this way:

This Is Going Great. You're laughing and making googly eyes at each other; you have the same interests and passions; you think you might already love him. He's even moved to sit next to you instead of across from you in the booth! In your head you've already paired your first name with his last name. His last name is something horrible like Gobbletron, but you don't care, you'll just be Iliza Shlesinger-Gobbletron and have tele-marketers forever dread having to pronounce your name. OMG DID OUR PINKIES JUST TOUCH!?

This Is Going Well. One of you is laughing more than the other, but you are having interesting conversation. You aren't overtly irritated by anything he's saying. Maybe he keeps mess-ing up his grammar, saying things like "could have went," but you write it off as some sort of colloquial affectation and maybe even envision that his rough-around-the-edges demeanor could complement your refinement.

This Is Going Fine. One of you keeps saying dumb things, and the other is trying to be polite. Nothing egregious has happened yet to make you leave. Maybe you noticed he is wearing those square-toed Kenneth Cole Reaction shoes from like ten years ago, but he's cute enough.

This Is Sparta! He has said something heinous about an ex, or children, or animals, or why Jews run the media. Maybe he even dared to utter something insane like, "I don't get why peo-ple choose to be gay." And now there's a fight, and you're two seconds away from sternum kicking him into a ditch.

So yeah, again, our date was . . . going somewhere between Well and Fine. I had finished my drink and was pondering a second one when this exchange transpired:

ILIZA: Do you have any pets?

DUDE: I have—well, *had*—a dog.

ILIZA: Aw, did he die?

DUDE: No, I sort of lost him in a breakup.

ILIZA: That's terrible. How long ago?

DUDE: A year.

ILIZA: Oh wow, were you together for a while?

DUDE: Nine years.

ILIZA: Uh. . . . Shot in the dark: Were you married?

DUDE: Yeah, we were.

ILIZA: Another shot in the dark. . . . Do you have kids?

DUDE: Yeah, I have two. They're six and nine.

Now. If someone is divorced, in my book that's not a reason to write him off. No, I like to write men off for concrete flaws like yawning weird or holding a fork the wrong way or saying "porridge." But the fact is I don't want to date a man with kids at this stage in my life. I like children fine, and I'm sure I'll love my own someday. But they add a layer of complication to a relationship that I'd just rather not deal with. Some women in my shoes might have opted to stick around and have that second drink. Their Girl Logic might have kicked in and insisted they hold onto a shred of hope, as in: "Hey, you never know! Maybe I'll fall in love with this 6 out of 10 *and* his adorable kiddos! And, at thirty-three, I can TOTALLY put my dreams aside to become a stepmom and be mildly resented by his children and hated by his wife who is FOR SURE only a few years older than me!"

My Girl Logic, on the contrary, went in the opposite direction. I immediately scanned through all the other things I could have done that night. This was my first night off in weeks! I did my makeup (I even contoured!), took an Uber, and wasted over an hour of my time with someone who wasn't even viable for me—something I could have known BEFORE WE'D EVEN MET if he'd bothered to tell me. Tomorrow I would be back on set; tonight could have been the start to something important or fun or silly, and I'm trying to find a boyfriend, and this guy is in the way, and I flat-ironed my hair for this, which is a nightmare in and of itself because my hair BREAKS EASILY! OH MY GOD MY HAIR IS ALL GONNA BREAK OFF AND WHEN I FINALLY MEET SOMEONE I LIKE I WILL JUST HAVE A HEAD OF BROKEN BLONDE PICKUP STICKS! I NEED TO GET AN ARGAN OIL HAIR MASK ON THE WAY HOME, IS CVS EVEN OPEN?! That whole Girl Logic thought stream happened in about five seconds. Then I stopped sweating, the room's ambient sound returned around me, and I made a choice. At the end of it, I decided to put myself first, simply saying:

ILIZA: Sorry, I'm not down with that.

DUDE: Huh? That's a little blunt—

ILIZA: It's not personal. I just don't want to date a man with kids. I want someone I can take vacations with without worrying about anyone else's schedule.

DUDE: Maybe you'd like them, though. . . .

ILIZA: Would you date me if I had two sons?

DUDE: No.

ILIZA: Wow, you answered that fast. Anyway, you seem like a nice guy, but by not putting "proud father of two" in your profile, you're hiding something. And even though I'm not into kids, there are so many women out there who are. Like I have one friend who is a few years older than me who would love to date a man with kids.

DUDE: Well, you're the oldest woman I've ever gone out with. [*Ouch.*]

ILIZA: Eh, whatever. You're a year out of a nine-year marriage, and you don't know what you want. Why would I date you?

DUDE: Huh?

ILIZA: I make a lot of money and I'm not ugly. Why would I want to put up with your baggage?

DUDE: Well, we could always hang out and see where it goes. . . .

ILIZA: You mean just fuck? No, I don't have a problem finding someone to sleep with.

DUDE: Guess you aren't gonna have that second drink? . . .

ILIZA: No, no I'm not. But you can walk me out. Oh, also?
This is why I don't give out my number.

And . . . *unmatch.*

Fun tangentially related anecdote that I'm leaving right here because, well, it's too cringeworthy a story not to put SOMEWHERE in this book. I had gone on about three dates with a guy—we'll call him Chris Hemsworth. OK fine, let's just call him Chris. He didn't look like Chris Hemsworth, though, so we'll call him Paul, not as in Walker, as in Giamatti. We'll call him a hot Paul Giamatti. HPG and I hadn't slept together. We had made out twice—*while standing,* in case you were curious on logistics. HPG looked like a boyfriend. Nice face, a little bit of softness on his body, but definitely not fat. He was funny and carried with him the kind of pain that can only come from feeling less than in the eyes of one's father. He was the kind of guy who, in conversation, you could see was thankful for a woman he could open up to. He was sweet and sensitive, which is why the next part of the story was such a shame.

One night, I decided to send HPG a pic of some underboob (no face; this isn't amateur hour!). Just a picture of my chest with a shirt pulled up enough that you could see my underudder. It was pretty hot. And I'm not going to lie—I sent it because I wanted to get a reaction. Isn't that what any sexy selfie is about? We want dudes to have a seizure and realize that there has never been a more perfect woman on the planet. We want their dicks to fly off and tears to roll down their faces (probably because their dicks just flew off?). Point is, I was just a girl . . . standing in front of a boy (and by boy I mean mirror with my phone in my hand) asking him to love her (i.e., to tell her that her body made him want sex with her that she would only bestow upon him when the right amount of alcohol had been consumed).

What he wrote back was . . . not what I expected:

"Me likey that picture long time."

Take a second to say that phrase out loud, as an adult. Let's forget the bastardization of an already overused *Full Metal*

Jacket quote. In my world, "me likey" comes eerily close to the reaction a toddler has when his mommy asks if he's enjoying his num-nums.

I stood there for a minute, and I guess I thought about it too long, because shortly another text came rolling in: "Herro? Why you no like meeee?"

And then he added . . . the cherry on the infantilized jargon sundae . . . a crying emoji.

That was our last text exchange. My Girl Logic tried to pretend, for a mere .13 seconds, that maybe I could still date him. But my libido had instantly withered when I received those texts, and whatever fantasy I'd been building up about HPG had been crushed by a giant toddler foot.

I'm sure not everyone would have reacted how I did. (Dirty baby-talk isn't my thing, but maybe it's yours?) And maybe HPG was a great guy at heart! But in that moment, when I decided to stop texting him, my GL was acting on my own best interests. Instead of instilling self-doubt, this time my GL was egging me on, telling me to cut and run, reminding me that in the past, whenever people have said dumb or weird things right off the bat, it's been an indicator of what's to come. How can a smart person *not* apply past lessons to current situations?

I decided a long time ago that just because I'm talking to a guy doesn't mean I have to try to make a relationship work (a.k.a. settle) if it doesn't feel right. No matter what age I am! I get it; as we grow older, it feels harder and harder to find a man we're remotely interested in. When you do manage to apple-bob your way to a decent human, you're so exhausted from trying that your Girl Logic starts thinking, "He's not *amazing,* but what if he's the last man who will ever want me? I *am* thirty-three. It's either make it work with him and be 64 percent happy or die alone wearing wedges with boot-cut jeans, alone in Valley Village. Guess I can overlook the fact that he says 'should have ate' instead of 'should have eaten,' picks his teeth at the table, and always forgets to ask me how my day was."

But it's OK that grammar matters to you. It's OK to want someone who doesn't pick his teeth and someone who is communicative. Your GL is picking up on the little things that are genuinely important to you because in the end they're not so little. In the end, they represent bigger things that can have a major impact on your long-term compatibility and happiness. Love and relationships are a fucking minefield of cheap shoes, selfish intentions, OK-looking bodies, and weird interpersonal issues. . . . And then there's the second date. GL might get tripped up at times, but at its heart it *knows* what will and won't work for you in the long term.

GL will eventually remind you of these truths: Could you die alone? Probably. Will you turn thirty, shit the bed, and never date again? No. Every time I get out of a serious relationship, I think, "I can't believe I have to start all over again. I'll never find a connection as special as the one I had with that guy." And then, one day, I find myself out with someone wonderful, and it all starts again.

Seriously, what does "having it all" even mean? "All" is subjective. Not every woman's vision of a perfect future looks the same. Not every woman wants kids. Not every woman wants to get married. Not every woman wants a house in the suburbs. Not every woman wants a career. Not every woman is attracted to men in the first place. Why and how did dudes become the key to our Perfect Future?

My friend, a gorgeous doctor, is married with two kids. She appears to have it all. And for her, she does—she has the life she wants, one that fulfills her. But her fantasy life is not mine. Even if I had the dream husband and all the rest, even if my love life were a 15 on a scale of 1 to 10, if I couldn't get on stage and talk about my experiences, your experiences, and the experiences of every woman we know, I wouldn't possess *my* version of having it all. My friend's life may look enviable because it's traditional; women haven't been independent long enough for us to totally abandon the ideal of being the trifecta of perfect wife, mother, and career woman (while still looking good). But ask yourself: If you couldn't do the thing you loved most, would you truly feel complete? If I couldn't express myself and make people laugh for a living, I would crumble inside. So I make sure I can keep doing what I love, for as long as I love doing it. Nothing is as important to me, for now.

How many women buy into this fantasy that every part of us should be eternally perky and shiny and soft, and that will help us "land a man" and get our wizened eggs fertilized, and then, finally, the dream will be realized!

Some women achieve that dream and discover it's a nightmare. Especially when husbands demand their own brand of perfection. I remember once, during their separation, the asshole husband of one of my close girlfriends said, "I'd want to sleep with you if you tanned more." Forget the inanity of this statement for a second. It's this type of standard—men wanting you to be something you're not—that's damaged so many women so much. If it wasn't the tan, it would be weight, or the way she spoke, or the clothes she wore. I feel bad that he was raised in a world where that sentence could even cross his mind. (They have now been divorced about three years. She is in her early forties, and her new fiancé is thirty-two. I love this ending.)

In our grandmothers' era, perfection meant looking pretty and keeping house. Women *had to be* good cooks because we weren't supposed to have jobs outside the home. Men wanted a woman who would stay home, vacuum in pearls, and then, after spending all day speaking *only to her baby,* she'd be expected to make dinner, have a martini ready, and blow him before retiring in her separate bed (no cuddling, even!?). So at some point, women in the '60s and '70s turned to pharmaceutical "helpers" like Valium to get through it all: the cooking, the cleaning, the demands, the expectations, the loveless marriages, the requisite blow jobs. (Hence the popularity of that Rolling Stones song "Mother's Little Helper.")

To me, the modern equivalent of Valium is white wine. Over the past several years, women's consumption of white wine has skyrocketed. The archetype of the blue-blooded American Wasp and her drink of choice, a symbol of breezy fun thinly veiling an underlying alcohol addiction, has become a mainstay in our pop cultural lexicon. Real Housewives drink it on camera, funny girls drink it in comedy and sketches,

Cougar Town made it a character, Hoda and Kathie Lee chug it to endure morning television.

I'm all for getting drunk on a weekend, or a Tuesday night if I don't have anywhere to be the next day. But the amount of alcohol single women are drinking these days seems a little excessive—and it makes me wonder if we're just using it as a numbing tool to escape the pain of our constant quest for a "perfect" life . . . *and* as a way to beat our own GL into submission. I've done it; everyone does it. You drink to deliberately lower your guard, your standards, your underwear. I've been out with someone I was half-attracted to and figured, "Whatever, we'll get fucked up, then kissing him will be fun." The other person, of course, never knows you're dulling your senses to find him attractive. Our GL may even turn optimistic: "What if I get drunk, we mess around, it turns out fun, and I actually grow to *like* this Hunchback?"

But maybe part of us is trying to quiet the voice inside us that actually *knows* what we want and deserve from love. Maybe we're so afraid we won't get it that we just have a drink, go along for the ride with whatever dude happens to be there, and take our chances. In college, heavy drinking made us more likely to hook up with guys we wouldn't normally be attracted to; as adults grappling with the realities of aging, alcohol can cause us to be more willing to take a chance on men we KNOW (or would know if were sober enough) aren't what we're looking for.

(And yes, of course women also drink just for fun because thinned blood feels good flowing through your body and drunk dancing is the best.)

Alcohol and GL don't always mix, though, especially in your twenties (also known as the grossest decade of one's life). Back then, I remember feeling outright ashamed when I'd make eye contact with a hot guy, like I should *apologize* for not being pretty enough for him. My ideal relationship fantasy then involved traditionally hot men; the hotter the better. And though I never did anything I didn't want to do, being blinded by the fact that an attractive man could desire me *did* lead me to make some poor romantic choices in my twenties. Really, for much of my life I was no better than those nerdy, newly rich dorks who develop apps or sell scripts and only date women who resemble wax figurines (perhaps to compensate for never getting laid in high school?). This didn't always end well for me.

When I moved to LA at twenty-one, I met a guy at the grocery store. Aw, just like in the movies! He had a chiseled jaw and a southern accent, and his name was Jason. We spoke for a bit, and he eventually called over his brother, Riley. Both of them were super hot, just mountains of proportionate muscle and tank tops. The three of us hung out for a few months and did everything together. I preferred Jason over Riley because he was softer, quieter, with less of a creep vibe.

Later that year—this was New Year's Eve 2005—I had to go back to Boston to retrieve some things from school, and I decided to spend NYE with Michelle. Hanging with her, I noticed that something felt off in my body. Welp, turns out I was pregnant. And yeah, it was Jason's. I was young and partnerless, not fully rooted yet, and my dreams for my life were far from fulfilled. I was not ready to have a child, and certainly not with this random dude I'd met at the Albertson's soup aisle. Hence, I wanted my pregnancy to be, well, *gone* as soon as possible.

It was the holidays, so we couldn't see a non-ER doctor *or* get to Planned Parenthood. I was scared, so I called my mom. This woman had paid for my college, sent me around the world, and supported me in moving to Los Angeles. Now I was calling to inform her that there was a good chance I was about to ruin all the hard work we'd put in because I was a sucker for some good old boy with a pretty face. What an ignorant, terrified brat.

She wasn't angry, though. She was understanding and warmly pragmatic. When I got back to LA, I called and discovered it was $600 for an abortion at Planned Parenthood. I called Jason and told him what was going on. "I want you to keep it," he said. "I won't help pay for an abortion."

I was making under $30K a year and supporting myself, so $600 was a huge chunk to me. I was lucky: my mother gave me the money. I think about that number a lot, and how insanely fortunate I was to have a mom who supported me, both emotionally and financially. There are so many women in my position who get pregnant and through lack of resources, end up giving birth to a child they can't care for—or, worse, hurting themselves trying to get an abortion from someone shady. This is part of why I support Planned Parenthood, because I'm not just a donor, I was once a patient.

After I flew home to LA and had the procedure, Jason stopped by the next day to see how I was feeling. For the record, I was feeling fine, and I had nothing to say to him. He told me he

(*Top*) My mother and me in 1986, in case my mom's sweater didn't give the year away.

(*Left*) Michelle and me at the pool, outside of something that we used to call a 1-hour photo. Ask your parents what that is.

(*Right*) Michelle and me in 2003. We had both just gotten off work at our summer jobs—I was a waitress at a place that still allowed customers to smoke cigarettes indoors. Here we're waiting outside for the fake-ID store in Irving, Texas, to open.

(*Above*) 1992. Dad and Barbara's wedding. As you can tell from the picture, I was totally cool with divorce.

(*Left*) 1993. Playing with leather scraps from my dad's factory.

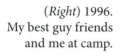

(*Right*) 1996.
My best guy friends
and me at camp.

(*Above*) 2001. The only girl in my high school improv troupe.

(*Left*) Andriana and me in 2004, on Semester at Sea. Nowadays she is just as tan, but my face is less full.

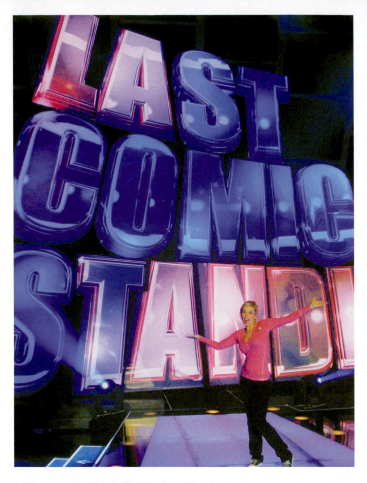

Man Up and Act Like a Lady

(*Above*) 2008. The night I won Last Comic Standing. Pretty sure they legally had to make the logo half pink because there was a girl in the competition.

(*Left*) Around 2010. This was my self-funded and self-released album—before Netflix did specials. *Permission granted by Robyn Van Swank.*

About 2014. Twice now I've been honored to perform with the USO for our troops in Afghanistan. This trip was with the *Today* show. It was Jay Leno, Al Roker, Craig Robinson, Kevin Eubanks, and me. *Permission granted by Fred Greaves.*

As a comic, you jot down jokes or keywords on whatever scrap you can find. I've even written sets on gum wrappers. This ancient set is from my first few years in comedy. I remember a few of these jokes but it mostly just reads like a crazy person's grocery list.

(*Above*) I met Mayim at the "Elle Women in Comedy" event. I did stand-up in front of a room of Hollywood's most important women in comedy. I couldn't believe that afterward, her publicist asked if she could meet me. I couldn't believe she knew who I was, let alone that she was a fan. We've been friends ever since. Here we are at my 34th birthday party. I told everyone the theme was "gothic" and Mayim was the only one smart enough to correct me and said, "Gothic is a style of architecture; Goth is how you want people to dress." I was like, "Well, let's hope no one misunderstands and comes dressed as a cathedral."

(*Left*) This is Jodi and me at one of a billion birthday parties we've attended together. Fun fact about women: We all love photo booths. She calls me "Mew" and I call her "JoJo."

I adopted Blanche around 2010, so I would have a dog to take on the road with me. I wanted a companion. The day I got her, I looked at her and said, "I don't have the time to train you, so just be cool," and she was. She sleeps entire plane rides, loves to be there, and is virtually always silent unless she is alone—then she freaks out. She just wants to always be included. Since I got her, she has traveled by my side to almost every single gig. We do everything together. Now we are to the point where she has her own fans. It warms my heart to see how excited people get to meet her at my shows. I just love sharing her beauty with the world. She is an angel and improves the life of anyone she touches. Blanche has a permanent sad/terrified look on her face. She's fine. After this show, about fifteen people brought her treats and gifts. She has a good life.

I think this picture perfectly encapsulates my image: all black, very tight pants, dope sneakers, and I'm sort of always hunched over, talking about something feminist or whimsical. *Credit: DJ Trauma*

was probably moving home to Arkansas, and I couldn't have cared less.

I did feel stupid, though. I couldn't help being physically attracted to someone pretty, but I definitely let Jason's looks—and what I thought his looks meant about me—override my better judgement. I was twenty-one and drunk. I was a fucking moron. My story is just one example of why women's reproductive health options are so important: in my case, it was because *all people make mistakes, but young people make more mistakes.*

Enough years have passed that I'm no longer struck dumb by hotness—in fact, when a super-good-looking guy asks me out, I immediately assume he's less smart, makes less money than me, and is otherwise severely flawed. I'm not always wrong about that, either. In your early thirties and up, if you're a man who is model hot, you're either already married, famous, or successful. If not, in my book you've sort of failed. I see it on dating apps all the time: these thirty-five-year-old male "models" have no education, no job, and poor social skills to boot. When you're a white dude with every possible societal advantage at your disposal, and you *still* can't figure your life out, then you're just dumb. And no, glomming on to your friend's "fitness brand" or throwing "social media consulting" onto the same resume as anything to do with real estate doesn't count as a career. (P.S. To the sole dilettante genius stunner whose brains have allowed him to pursue pottery, snorkeling, a clothing company, and a medical practice on the side: Comedy is about sweeping generalizations. Don't be a stickler.)

Another damning element of constantly striving for a perfect fantasy is that we expect perfection, then mock women
who fall short of it. If someone gets work done on their face or
body and it's great, we'll never know. But if they get it done
wrong, even slightly, they end up looking . . . weird. Not bad,
necessarily, just . . . they're in the Uncanny Valley. The "Uncanny Valley" is a term used in robotics (I can't believe I'm
typing a sentence about robotics) when an android or robot is
meant to look like a human and comes close, but something is
still off enough to make you feel uneasy.

So how can we stop fruitlessly trying to squeeze our lives
into constrictive little Disney-princess boxes? How can we stop
letting ourselves slowly morph into white-wine-addled robots
in the name of "perfection"? Remember that whole "having it
all" thing I mentioned earlier—how my friend's version of "all"
was nowhere near the same as my own? That's true for everything, and, honestly, the only person you need to impress is
yourself. I know that sounds schmaltzy and is easier said than
done. It's hard to accept yourself, and it's hard when it seems
like everyone around you has what you want. (Why don't we
stop to think that maybe we have what they want?)

Sometimes, your GL whispers so many things at once, you
become numb. A great example of this is whenever I give myself too much time to get ready to go out. I'm guaranteed to
find new imperfections that don't exist, thereby adding more
and more layers of crap to my face and ultimately ending up
looking uglier in the process. (Ladies, give yourself forty-five

minutes to get ready, tops. Contouring alone is insane; why do all of our faces have to look like Picasso's cubist period?)

Other times I stop all the fretting and just accept myself out of exhaustion. My GL helps me reprioritize and remember what I'm really looking for, and I just stop trying—not in a bird's-nest-on-my-head, no-teeth-brushing kind of way, but in an "I AM ENOUGH, I'VE HAD ENOUGH!" way.

Look in the mirror and concede. Let GL's internal chaos hone itself down into the simple, truest version of you: "I'm just gonna wear these heels, and fucking who cares." You'll go out into the night, and you'll realize that all the fretting and self-loathing wasn't worth it because (A) no man could possibly know all the effort you put in and (B) everyone else is only paying attention to themselves, anyway. In the end, we're all only trying to look good so we can get that one good Instagram picture. And maybe that one perfect husband because he saw your one good Instagram picture? Whatever.

6

How to Text a Man
Without Throwing Your Phone
Through a Window

We've already discussed how dating and sex can drive women mad. But no other form of personal interaction can send our Girl Logic further off the deep end than texting. I mean, is there ANYTHING that provokes a more classic GL response (obsessing over subtext, daydreaming over future possibilities, and ruminating over yesterday's heartbreaks) than texting? Our parents don't understand this, of course. My mom always says, "Why don't you pick up the phone and call him?" And I'm like, "Because I'm not a psychopath." Phone calls are for family, doctors, and American Airlines telling you that your flight is delayed.

Most of us have spent our dating careers poring over texts from guys, analyzing perceived inflection: "He used an ellipsis—was there something else he wanted to say? Something he wanted me to think? Is he trapped inside his own brain? Is this a *Diving Bell and the Butterfly* situation?! DOES HE NEED SAVING?!"

We've created stories: "He texted during lunch because he OBVIOUSLY remembered that I like eating lunch." We've plotted the perfect response, but only after conducting an informal Gallup poll: "53 percent of my girl friends think I should write back 'k,' while 47 percent believe I should say 'OK' with a smiley face, after exactly three hours."

Our Girl Logic kicks in as a self-preservation device, both to help us explain the unexplainable and to bring rationality to something that feels beyond our control. Even when it comes to a simple text, we are factoring in past relationships, current feelings, and our hopes for the guy down the road—sex, a relationship, or just a timely reply.

This stuff is more confusing than ever because my generation of daters has created a world where *no one* is human. We're all just text boxes floating in space, and it's so damned easy to walk away from someone who appears to be nothing more than binary code with perceived inflection. Guys and girls meet on apps, start flirting over text, and three lines in, they just . . . wander away forever. In real life you'd never say, "Hey, what are you doing tonight?" (asking at like, 6 p.m., rude) and then stroll off to follow a butterfly instead of waiting for an answer. But we've created a world of romantic interactions where this is completely normal. We ignore, we ghost, and above all else, we *just keep looking for something better.*

To cope with all the crap, modern women have begun to, well, act like men. Act like we don't give a fuck, like we're "chill," like we're into "ethical nonmonogamy" and playing games and waiting fucking forever to respond to a message. Can you blame us? Hell, a lot of guys sign up for dating apps just for the satisfaction of "matching" with a girl, then they never bother talking to her. For this reason, we've stopped being honest about how we feel and what we want. We've given in to Girl Logic when it tells us to play games, wait hours to respond, or act like we have sixteen men waiting in the wings on a Friday night. In short, we've started giving back exactly what we started getting: nothing.

Because texting is so nuanced, I figured I'd help you through it. I happen to pride myself on being one of the world's best texters. Not only am I great with inflection and punctuation, I'm also the fastest texter you'll ever meet. Plus, my interest level is obvious. I don't like you, it's clear. If I want something, I say it (of course I'd prefer you just guessed it until I change my mind; I'm a woman, after all).

This chapter is your very own guide to texting men without losing your mind. I'll show you how to better understand guys, show you when Girl Logic can be used to your advantage, and explain when it's necessary to turn off GL altogether as you attempt to communicate with people who have penises. Basically, I'm gonna try to show you how to not feel awful at the end of a text exchange.

Five Modern Male Archetypes . . . and How to Text Them

The following archetypes don't represent ALL men out there, but most likely *do* encapsulate a few you've encountered in the wild. Here I'll explain each man's texting style and what to do and not do if you're trying to date one of these guys. I'd like to stress that there are lots of nice, normal, wonderful guys out there, but since they are all the aforementioned superlatives, you don't need a guide for them.

1. The Entrepreneur with a Good Heart . . . but No Brain

This guy is good-looking but hasn't quite found himself. He might own a T-shirt brand that spreads awareness about "inner peace" or an energy drink / bracelet combo that helps raise money for poor kids in the rain forest. Problem is, while he seems like a philanthropist, only time will tell if he's a successful one. Meanwhile, you have to hear him prattle on endlessly about this one "amazing summer he and his best girlfriend backpacked through Honduras." You'll run into him again in ten years and he'll be married with at least one baby. The wife will be mind-numbingly supportive and either be a stunning Latina or a really average white woman; there is no in between for men like this. His millionaire dreams will either be realized, or he will have moved back to Mariana's hometown to be closer to her family.

His Texting M.O.: "To just reach out! Just spreadin' the love!" He'll send these short missives just to check if you're still responsive. He might even say something as trite as "What's up pretty lady?"

What to Text If You're Trying to Ask Him Out: Creative types like this are a little scattered, so if you are the kind of girl who doesn't wanna play a game, be as direct as possible: "Hey, I'm going to rob a bank on Saturday, want to come?" Offer something a few days ahead of time, because he will never be able to get his shit together day of. If he can't find the time and doesn't offer an alternative plan, move on. This guy is a headache.

What to Text If You Want to Blow Him Off: Nothing. He'll move on of his own accord because he is so busy donating a portion of his maca gummy snack proceeds to an online eco fashion show.

Pitfalls to Look Out For: Guys like this often seem . . . busy. They aren't trying to be assholes; they're just really consumed with their projects. So he might engage in a conversation for an hour, drop out, and then a day later text at like 3 p.m. with, "Hey chica! You lovin' life today?" Also, he might not wear shoes.

2. Youth Pastors (a.k.a. That Charming Small-Town Everyman Type)

OK, so these men might not be *actual* youth pastors because how many of us encounter youth pastors regularly? Basically, these are small-town guys who know everyone, get along with everyone, and find themselves incredibly charming. Often these guys take society's overwhelmingly positive response to their existence as their cue to get into acting or some kind of public speaking or performing. They are attractive, charismatic, and love to talk. Public speaking, whether you're trying to be funny, commanding, or impactful, is often done for one reason, though: to serve the speaker's ego. Think about it; you have this innate desire to stand in front of strangers and have them listen to you. In small towns, an audience can be hard to come by, except if you attend church. "Oh, you wanna serve the Lord? Well, let's get you an audience!" Eventually, some of those guys move to Los Angeles with hopes of turning that passion for public speaking into a less secular endeavor, like . . . acting. Or hosting. Which is what actors do when they can't get acting work. I would know, I've done it twice.

His Texting M.O.: He's straightforward; if he wants to see if you're around, he'll try to pin down a concrete plan. Nothing nefarious.

What to Text If You Want to Ask Him Out: "You around this week?" This is good because it gives him a chance to talk about / show off all the things he is doing, and he still feels like he is in control when he then suggests a plan on a day that works for him. Remember, he is a failed public speaker trying to get famous; he needs to be in control of something in his life.

What to Text If You Want to Blow Him Off: Tell him you need to focus on your career. He will understand that, and then he'll tell you he has to do the same.

Pitfalls: Might have an ego, an ex-wife (from when he got small-town married at like eighteen), and might be naïve to city life. Also calls all dudes "brother," but he's white.

3. Bad Boys

There's no such thing as a free spirit after age twenty-one. "Bad boys" are just irresponsible adults who behave like children. Maybe they do drugs, maybe they're emotionally unavailable, but the whole charade becomes a little ridiculous because they're old and they have nothing left to rebel against. Breaking the law (I'm talking armed robbery, not buying weed) just makes you a criminal. And tattoos? Not edgy anymore; most people have them. Oh, you had a famous tattoo artist do that $500 thing on your bicep? Is it a frying pan? Dope. Oh you wear a leather jacket and drink and don't always text back? Guess that makes me a bad boy, too!

His Texting M.O.: To see if you are around to fuck. (You don't need me to explain this one to you.) He doesn't wanna hear something cute or funny about your mom visiting.

What to Text If You Want to Ask Him Out: If you wanna be as casual as him, "You around later?" will always pique his interest. You can't ask if he's around now because he probably has a day job he likes to pretend doesn't exist, like managing a chain restaurant or a Goorin Bros.

What to Text If You Want to Blow Him Off: Nothing. He's a bad boy; he won't care. Even if he does care, it won't matter because he's spent so much time trying to look like he doesn't.

Pitfalls: He might become a vegetable when he crashes his "hog." He might have a thumb ring or bad hair under that beanie he wears in the summer. Filthy fingernails. He also, unless blessed with good genetics, might have weird teeth.

4. Older but Trying

At some point in your early twenties, you will meet an older guy. He might not be attractive or wealthy, but he's mature. He has manners, a mortgage, and he knows who to call when there's a problem with health insurance. Really, if you met this man when you were older, you wouldn't be impressed. But when you're twenty-three and he's thirty-five, and he knows who to "deal with at the airline," it's hot. I once dated an older guy who would pick me up for our date, pull up to my apartment, and stand outside his car with the doors open. What a move! In hindsight, dude should have come to the door; plus, he was driving a truck in LA and didn't work in the farming industry; weird choice. (Also, that was the guy who later pretended he died, so that explains a lot, but even I couldn't have predicted a death faking to happen.)

His Texting M.O.: He is genuinely trying to ask you out. He wants to take you on a date; maybe it's to have sex, maybe he likes you, but still. A date!

What to Text If You Want to Ask Him Out: You won't have to. He will ask you. Older guys are great like that.

What to Text If You Want to Blow Him Off: Call, don't text—older guys just don't text as well as younger women do. His old-man fingers won't be able to respond fast enough! These men need a simple, straightforward phone call explaining that you're sorry but you just HAVE TO wash your hair tonight (that's something they'll remember from their youth).

Pitfalls: Children your age, glares in public, old-man body, old-man smell. Might make you watch *Fletch.* Has a collection of Robert Graham shirts that won't quit.

5. *So Hot You Could Actually Cry*

Once in awhile you get a guy so perfect that, even on your best day, you wonder if you shouldn't be hobbling along in front of him, periodically bowing down to throw rose petals in his path. Jeans slung low, worn-in leather belt, dog tag–ish necklaces hanging (necklaces you'd like to imagine an old gypsy woman gave him when she cursed him with terrible beauty, but in reality they're from an Army surplus store). Maybe he has long hair, and every time you run your hands through it you think, "There's no way the man I end up marrying is gonna have hair, so I'd better get these pets in now." Maybe he's just jacked, and, when he wears a Henley (because you bought him one and threw out his other clothes), he makes you feel like you're living in the Abercrombie ads of your youth. Regardless of his particular type of hotness, guys like this are but a fleeting dream for any hypermotivated or smart woman. Yes, arm candy is fun to flit around with, but, at the end of the day, you don't want to hear his songs he plucked out on bass, you don't want to hear his fitness ideas, and he probably watches *Ballers* or cheers for The Ohio State, and you're like, "You didn't even go there." Complex women need complex men.

His Texting M.O.: He wants to ask you out. But he's shy and doesn't give long answers. Don't take his silence as a slight. He is just kind of quiet, and/or stupid.

What to Text to Ask Him Out: A guy like this enjoys a direct woman. Ask him to meet for a drink. Remember, he's hot. He's gonna want, like, whisky, so don't take him to a bar with embarrassing drinks in pineapples.

What to Text If You Want to Blow Him Off: Just tell him you have to study.

Pitfalls: Might not know current events. Might *think* he knows current events, but, um, he only reads tweets. Will absolutely have an ex-girlfriend who is hotter than you; don't let him know it bothers you.

How to Decipher a Dude-Text

Now let's decipher a classic text response from a guy. Let's say you send this message to a new guy you're seeing: "Hey, stupid meeting ran late. I'm running 20 minutes behind, but I'm on my way!"

"OK": Variations on a Theme

If he writes back "OK!" it means he doesn't mind and is pumped to see you. No stress, no drama.

If he writes back "ok," don't read into it one moment further. He's a dude, and he got the text. End of story.

If he writes back "k," you might need to worry a little. Both of you know by now that "k" is the international text sign of passive-aggressive approval. NO ONE DOESN'T KNOW THAT "K" IS SOMETHING YOU WRITE WHEN YOU'RE MIFFED. If they don't know that? Then you need to date someone else because lack of awareness about social practices, especially when it comes to texting, will manifest itself in other annoying ways later. Dude lives under a rock; probably a rock in his parents' house. In sum: he's mildly annoyed you're late, and he half-assedly wants to make you feel bad on your lonely little ride over there.

If he writes back "k . . . " (NOTE THE ELLIPSIS!) then he is a fucking serial killer, and do not go to that bar. The subtext of this ellipsis is "It's OK . . . but not really." It creates unease and makes you think he's holding something back—something he should have spit out. Or maybe he simply has no idea how to use an ellipsis, and do you really want to date an idiot who doesn't know his punctuation:;'!]?

Rules for Text-Ghosting

Rule 1: You can't ghost if you've been out more than twice in two weeks. A bond has been established, you liked them enough to have another go, now you're more than strangers. You owe them a text.

Rule 2: You can't ghost if you've slept with the person (and it wasn't the first night you met).

One-night stands are as much of a part of dating as guns are a part of American culture; it's impossible to separate the two, despite all the downsides.

Rule 3: You can't ghost if you're in the middle of an actual discussion via text. Have the social decency to at least end the conversation, don't be a weirdo. All else is fair—not cool, but fair.

The Ghosting Grace Period: If you go out once and you aren't into him, ghosting in the first twenty-four hours should be considered your grace period. If a guy disappears, only to text a girl three days later, then he's just rude and obviously doesn't think you're that great. Guys, listen to me now. If you like a girl, it behooves you to text her the next day to say, "That was fun, let's hang this weekend." Unless you're the president, you have time. And if you don't? "Hey, that was fun. I'm busy this weekend but when are you free again?" is perfect.

How to Text a Hookup Gone Awry

Once upon a time, I dated this guy. We went out maybe five times over the course of a few weeks. By this point we were texting every day. I thought it would be fun if he came to Las Vegas with me for a show. When I asked him and told him what weekend, he said, "Sounds fun," but never gave me a concrete yay or nay; in fact, he outright disappeared. Actually, he went camping.

He said, "I'm going camping," and I said, "Oh fun, where?" and . . . that was it. I guess what he meant was, "I'm going camping literally right now and could lose service at any second."

He resurfaced a few days later, but it was too late—I was already in Vegas, and I was already irritated as hell by his flakiness. If you ever find yourself in a similar situation, dealing with someone you're ACTUALLY DATING but who refuses to give you a straight-up answer about plans, your Girl Logic might start going haywire. You might be tempted to play it cool to mess with him. You might start having fears that if you don't respond in a sweet enough way, you'll scare him off AND WHAT IF HE WAS THE ONE?!?!?!? You can't let those GL-triggered fears consume you. You need to tell your GL to shut up and realize that what you really want is someone who doesn't act like this.

Here are a few options for what to say back:

- "Help, I'm in a Clark County prison and they've taken my shoelaces."

- "I'm already in Vegas under someone else right now. You snooze you lose, dork."

- "You made it weird, dude. If you're not into this, no problem."

That last one is what I wrote. I wanted to make it clear that he acted in an unattractive way and also give him an out. Sometimes men's eyes have to be opened to their selfish behavior. A threat that you will walk makes them step up or step out.

How to Handle an
Out-of-Nowhere Reconnection Text

I went on two dates with this guy once, and he was . . . OK. I couldn't tell if I was attracted to him, but he was nice enough. Not that great looking but somehow he *should have* been. You know, one of those people that has all the right features, but they just aren't working together properly? Good teeth, nice skin, good hair, good cheekbones . . . but still feels off? There's that Uncanny Valley again! But we've all felt it, and in those situations you almost get frustrated, asking yourself, "Why am I not attracted to this objectively attractive person?" (The worst is when you decide he isn't "cute enough for you," and then he starts dating a cool, pretty girl, and you're like, "Wow, maybe I missed something there.")

Anyway, point is, I wasn't magnetically attracted to him. Then we both went out of town and didn't communicate, which was fine, because again, Uncanny Valley. What *wasn't* fine was when he texted me *a month later* asking if I wanted to hang out again. Sometimes a lag can mean the guy's actually busy with work or a family crisis or a near-death experience, but in this case I got the impression he was sitting on the toilet, scrolling through his messages, noticed our old chain and was like "oh yeah, her." It made me feel super special. Since I was already erring on the side of "meh," I never wrote back. I'm convinced I wasn't the only girl he toilet-texted that day.

So if you find yourself going on a few dates with someone, only to not hear from him again for a month or two, here are your options:

1.   IGNORE. Listen to me on this. Nothing on this earth, not "I love you," not an orgasm—nothing feels better than the gratification that only grows over the hours when you resist texting someone back! It's like you can feel him squirming with anticipation. It gives you power! POWAH!

2.   Actually, there is no option 2. If you had even the slightest relationship with someone and he doesn't have the respect to let you know it's over? Don't waste your time building up his ego. Leave him be, look for other options, and do not cut your own hair.

When and How to Dump a Man via Text

Now, onto the much maligned text breakup. It's controversial, and I try not to do it unless it's deeply well deserved. Occasionally . . . it is.

If you found out your new boyfriend (like, of one month or less) is cheating on you, still entangled with an ex, or is otherwise a raging garbage fire who doesn't warrant a proper face-to-face or telephone conversation (maybe he keeps post-ing gym pics and #ing it with "GAINZZZZ"). Or if for what-ever reason you're livid, you're over it, you are watching him with binoculars anyway, send him a dump text saying some-thing short and sweet—"I've been thinking about it and I don't want to see you anymore. Byeeeeee." should suffice. Or if you have irrefutable evidence that he is a bad person, and you're feeling especially strong-willed, you could always text, "I know what you did." Drop the mic, and never pick it back up.

Also, a fried shrimp emoji is often enough to confuse a man away from you forever. ;)

How to Text the Guy
You Actually Want to Keep

When you really like someone, it can be scary. Especially as a modern woman having gone through the crazy emotional wringer most of us have suffered through in the name of "dat-ing." So when you find a man who's actually cool, and thoughtful, and smart, and shows up for you, God knows you REALLY want to keep him around. Your GL might tell you to try harder (I BAKED YOUR LUNCH INTO A PIE!) or be non-chalant ("I accidentally called you the wrong name and farted, whatevs."), but it's important to wear your heart on your sleeve. You need to let your guard down if you're ever going to let someone in.

Everything in our society tells us "DON'T LET A MAN KNOW YOU WANT A RELATIONSHIP! They are AFRAID!"

But ask yourself, do you want a guy who doesn't want to be with you? No. And there are plenty of normal men who *do* want relationships. So stop catering to what you think men want, and just be honest. Like, you want a boyfriend, right? But you want the right one, not just a scarecrow in Air Maxes. So write . . .

"I would like to date someone exclusively, but only if it's the right person. For now, I'm having fun meeting people and seeing what's out there." Something like this puts no pressure on him and lets him know you can be just as chill as him. If he acts like a tool because you said the word "exclusively" and he heard it out of context, that's his problem.

Of course, if you're already convinced THIS IS THE GUY FOR YOU and you don't *want* to "see what's out there," you might start internally freaking out, imagining your future kids, deciding who goes where for holidays. That's fine, but you cannot tell him you're thinking about any of this shit. Play it cool until you know for sure you're on the same page: "I'm having a great time with you and am excited to see where this goes" or some such. Don't rush anything, and maintain a normal pace. Feel it out, and, most importantly? Don't be the first to look crazy.

7

Sorry, I Can't Hear You over How Single You Are

Some women might be single because they're too demanding. Some are not super attractive, or they're rude. They might be too busy for a real relationship or have unrealistic expectations. I should know, I'm one of them. I once had a boyfriend say to me, "I'm sorry I'm not the perfect version of a man you invented in your head." And I retorted, "Not as sorry as I am! NOW HAND ME THAT PIZZA AND GET OUT OF MY TUB!"

Kidding, I was in the shower. But he was right. Girl Logic makes love difficult because there are so many types of men we can imagine ourselves with. Oh, you just want someone who will listen to you and love you for you? Then you get that, and you just want some dumb gorilla who will fuck you and be your arm candy. Then you want someone funny. Then you want a quiet smart guy. Then back to the gorilla—oops, he slipped on a banana, not so tough anymore.

Our Girl Logic clings to the past while racing toward the future. I've been single and caught myself crying out, "I JUST WANT A BOYFRIEND!" while chomping on Charleston Chews and watching *Frasier*. Then, when I started dating someone, I'd find myself thinking, "Wow, I really miss traipsing about Silver Lake and making out with that hot emotionally unavailable guy with three roommates; that was fun. I need to go to Vegaaaaas! It's Monday, let's do shots!"

This is great if you just want to date forever and you plan on drinking enough virgin blood to stay youthful. But eventually, you grow up. You get tired.

There are plenty of other women who are single only because they have standards. By the way, "your standards are too high" is someone's subtle way of saying that you want someone that brings more to the table than you are bringing yourself. There's no such thing as "too high" if you're exceptional! You think anyone ever told Leonardo DiCaprio his standards were too high?

It gets weirder when you're a successful, unmarried woman in entertainment. Your love life is considered public business, and fans and reporters don't even pretend to give a shit how you feel about your new project or your latest castmates. Nope, all they REALLY want to know is why you're single. You could be hanging off a cliff, one arm orangutaned above your head, holding on by the third finger on your left hand, but, before saving you, the fireman would demand to know why you're not wearing a ring.

We write books, hold hours-long conversations, and devote magazine columns to the loaded conundrum of women who are "single—now what?" "Top Activities to Try When You're Single," "Ways to Bond with Your Pet but Not Seem Weird," "Single and Ready to Eat Ham? Here's a Guide."

Apparently, singlehood is a terrible disease you should be very, very ashamed of. Everyone feels entitled to prod you about your singleness until they conclusively determine what's wrong in an effort to reassure themselves that they'll never catch your death stench of aloneness. Like you're gonna break down crying and confess, "OK FINE, I'M SINGLE BECAUSE I EAT MY COUCH CUSHIONS AND MAKE HORSE NOISES DURING SEX!"

Newsflash: men don't deal with this. There is no *Esquire* article called, "You're Single, Bro—Now What?" because the answer would be, simply, "Now I Can Go Back to Jerking off Whenever I Want. #Sandwich." (In fact, to research my claim, I googled "Esquire" and "single," and what came up was an article called "Why It's Great You're Single.")

And, yes, this happens to me, too. Not the couch-cushion and horse-noise thing. I'm talking about the questioning. I've been in meetings where men think it's OK to ask, "So are you single? When was your last relationship?" I'm stunned every time. Especially when the interrogator is a married man. I'm like, "I bet your wife would find this line of questioning SUPER relevant."

And the older you get, the worse it is: "Nobel Prize, huh? But who will you share it with? Have you tried ScienceMeet .com?" No one asks a twenty-two-year-old why she's single—for lots of us, your twenties are expendable, for figuring yourself out enough to start tackling the hard work of your thirties. In your twenties you can say stupid shit and date with abandon, be bad at your job, switch careers, move cities five times, get bangs, grow them out, get them again three years later; you can even try a clip-in nose ring. Point is, that's your time to mess around and not be judged. And if someone does judge you? Your go-to is, "I'm twenty-five! I just googled 'Electoral College'!"

Keep in mind, there is a difference between "*How* are you still single?" and "*Why* are you still single?" The former is a compliment, as in, "Wow, you're so amazing; how has someone not begged you to marry them?"

But "Why are you single?" feels like an accusation: "What the hell is wrong with you that you couldn't just pick someone who wasn't right for you and *make it work*? That's what adults DO." Um, sorry? I guess? Someone once posited that very idea to me on a popular podcast. "You dated *all these guys,* and you couldn't make it work with any of them?" As if there is a finite and predetermined amount of men a woman will ever have to work with; like the universe says, "We're gonna send you a jealous alcoholic, a pretty boy with no marketable skills, and a handful of other mediocre ways to settle. These will be your only options, so figure it out."

When you're single, you take great comfort in other single women, for one simple reason: they feel your pain. Sure, it's easy to commiserate about the assholes who don't text you back, but admit it—sometimes, deep down, you find yourself thinking, "I have no idea why I'm still alone. But HER, on the other hand, she has some issues."

I try not to heed my own Girl Logic, though, when it attempts to make me think petty thoughts about my friends. I've always been the kind of person who is happy for others' happiness. Weddings, relationships, whatever; I never felt other people's relationship status affected my own . . . until I was thirty-three, and I went through a period where I was dating and dating, to no avail, as every guy around me seemed to find new and unique ways to be terrible. With age, the more we grow and figure out what we will and won't stand for. So it stings even more when you find yourself being continually rejected. You've put in soooo much goddamn time and effort to become this amazing version of you. When a man seems to fault you for this, it can feel like an affront to the entire life you've created for yourself.

Also worth noting is that some women—like some men— are single because, well, they're kinda annoying. Does this mean they don't deserve love? No, it just means they shouldn't procreate. But you're not a bad person if you look at certain women who complain about their singledom and think, "Yeahhhhh, but you talk exclusively in a baby-voice and you think wearing a shirt that says 'DIVA' is cute."

Truthfully, the fact that her love life is ever even considered a factor when assessing a woman's character is antiquated, insulting, and irrelevant. So you're not a mom—does that mean you hate children? So you're divorced—does that mean you have no idea how to be in a relationship? So you don't have a boyfriend right this second—does that mean you're a used-up piece of fuck gristle! No. And yet, wherever we are in our love lives, whatever instantaneous snapshot people take of us, that's how we're judged. And what's worse, we internalize those judgments.

One of the main cultural messages we constantly get is that single women somehow aren't to be trusted. We're either sad-sack man-haters who eat our feelings, or we're threats who act like rogue spies and hang out at frequent-flyer lounges to steal yo' man.

EXHIBIT A: a few years ago my mother got the opportunity to teach an art class on a cruise ship. It was a great gig because she would teach one watercolor class a day, and, for that, she and a guest (me!) got to do a two-week luxury cruise for free. There was a couple there around her age: late fifties / early sixties. The husband was a bubbly, lovely man who *loved* to joke around with my mom, who's, as I've stated, awesome. I will never forget how, whenever she would talk to the man, if she touched his back in a friendly gesture, she would always touch the wife, too. She told me, "I always include her because I don't want her to think I'm flirting with him." (My mom isn't even single, but my stepdad wasn't with us.) She knew people might talk, that the wife might get jealous; we're just so used to the idea that women out in the world alone must be on the prowl or up to no good.

Relationships were easy in my twenties, because I deliberately jumped from one to another. It wasn't a fear of being alone as much as enjoying a steady stream of dudes who liked me. Then one day my love life stopped being so effortless. And no, it wasn't the moment I turned thirty, it's just that as you age, your options start to . . . taper off. (You also become more selective about who you spend your time with.)

People get married, including that one guy you kind of had on reserve; he meets some girl named "Allison," and they fall in love and move in together and get married at her parents' estate in Connecticut. Allison has a Pilates body and some adorably meaningful job you can't compete with, like curating a children's museum. She has no idea you ever existed, which is funny since you know that if you rang his doorbell tomorrow (do not ring his doorbell) and said, "Remember when we did mushrooms at that cabin in Big Bear in 2009 and you said you loved me? I know you still mean it," he would totally leave her. You know it in your heart, or at least you think you do. But don't go to their house. Stay here with me.

The Three Kinds of Single

But single women are not pathetic sad sacks or prowling man-eaters, as we all know. There are three kinds of single in my book:

Looking. Your Girl Logic tells you to constantly keep one eye open for the right guy—at the post office, at the bar, riding the subway, walking the dog. Hey, everyone's read the books and seen the meet cute movies. Your Girl Logic reminds you about all the random schmoes you know who met over a game of Jenga at a coffee shop or a shitty house party they almost decided to skip. Girl Logic yells, "Just go with no expectations and talk to everyone!" (But, um, having no expectations is hard because, fuck—you got dressed up, slapped on some fake tanner, and watched a Saudi Arabian girl's Instagram makeup tutorial on the perfect cat eye—no expectations? I *EXPECT* A GUY TO NOTICE!)

Your Girl Logic makes you think, "But if I don't put on a little makeup and look my best to run this inane errand, there's a slim but very real chance that I might miss out on meeting my one and only true-forever soul mate! He's gonna be in line at Trader Joe's, and we're both gonna be holding the same jar of Speculoos Cookie Butter, and *he'll just know*! And if I miss him, I'll never have a family, never achieve happiness, and never feel complete, and I will die alone surrounded by happy couples laughing at me. HOW AM I SUPPOSED TO REST WHEN LOVE IS ALWAYS JUST AROUND THE CORNER!?"

Anyone who's single is usually in looking mode. Ninety-nine percent of the time, if people say "they aren't looking for a relationship right now," it just means they're not looking for a relationship with you. For the most part, people don't knowingly pass up the perfect person. Going on dates, asking friends if they know anyone, attending events or parties you wouldn't normally care about—"who knows who might be there?!"—keeps you going.

Loving It. This is the kind of single euphoria you experience after you've emerged from something suffocating, lame, or just bad. You feel liberated; you want to fart freely, eat deli ham out of a bag, be a veggie on your couch, and not have to worry about that asshole you were having boring sex with. You wanna go out, make out, sleep with whatever you want. You're in personal satisfaction mode and it's a wonderful place to be. You make up a fraction of that 1 percent who truly, honestly aren't looking for a relationship.

The Lady Doth Protest Too Much. You never want to be this girl, but we've all been her at times. This is the one who can't stop telling everyone how much she looooooves being single; she will even tell it to men she's on a date with because she doesn't want to "scare him off." As if some men expect women to be like, "Sure! Let's just fuck and chill forever and, like, see what happens! Time isn't a thing! Babies can happen when I'm sixty! Aging skin is valued in our culture!"

Are women capable of being fine with being single? Of course! But when it's been a while and we can't find a partner, sometimes we half-heartedly resign ourselves to being single—adopting a passive-aggressive "fuck you" attitude toward the universe: "Oh, you meant for JUST ME to be miserable and alone? Ok cool. Then I'm not gonna bother because I know there's no one out there for me who isn't terrible. I'll just go live in a toad hole and disappear and make everyone happy!"

It's hard not to get a little bitter. People always seem to blame the girl for her own romantic misfortune, and they assume she's doomed if she happens to be uncoupled for a while. Is it possible that your ex-boyfriend was just shitty and you were smart enough to ditch him? Is it possible you're choosing to be alone for a while, either because you need to recover from something awful or because you actually like having time to do your own thing and watch a shit ton of TLC?

Just like the phases I listed above, there are phases of trying to come to terms with your own solitariness. It's like the grieving process. These phases can severely test your belief in a higher power or your sense of good and rightness in the world. It is hard to believe in karma when you see all these awful people around you finding love while you keep stuttering along on an endless lazy Susan of half-assed kisses and split checks.

Five Steps of Single Grieving

We've all had those breakups that we longed for and initiated, and woke up the next day thinking, "I'm free!!!" This list is for the other kind of breakup: when you're mourning a relationship you loved that felt like it was cut off in its prime.

Denial. Your GL tells you, "I'm single because I'm choosing to be," which is half true! But really what you mean is you're choosing not to settle and you are also not happy that what you had ended. Of course it will all be OK, but telling yourself it will be OK sort of denies that right now it fucking sucks, which is the truth—and also OK.

Anger. Your GL kicks into rageful comparison mode: "WHY! WHYYYYYYYYYY does that horrible bitch get a boyfriend and a beautiful shiny engagement ring and I'm still single? Her capped teeth don't even look like teeth! Why did Jamie sleep with every guy on Facebook and even sleep with a *married man,* and, as a reward for that, she gets a gorgeous husband who adores her, while I get stuck going on a date with some guy named Clark who wears too many leather bracelets and drives a Mini? It's a girl car! And for God's sake why is he so THIN?"

Bargaining. Your GL tries to talk you into why you should stay in. Like, all the time. "I need another night to regroup from not leaving the house." Or, the other way: "If I go out tonight, then I'll feel better about staying in tomorrow." Or it's like a movie/game: "OK, universe. I'm gonna go on thirty-seven dates in thirty-seven hours and if I don't find Mr. Right, then I'm going to stab myself thirty-seven times."

Depression. Your GL wants you to drag a sleeve of Thin Mints into a cave of self-loathing: "No one loves me. The world wants me to be alone. At least I have the toads who also live in this hole for company."

Acceptance. Your GL comes back around in all her glory. There's a spring in her step. You're ready to face the world again: "It is what it is. I'm gonna be fine. I have a date tomorrow!" See, your GL is on your side again. All of this obsessive thinking and ruminating finally burned away everything that wasn't essential and helped you focus on what's important and what's real.

Similarly, women who find themselves single in their thirties come up with various rationalizations to explain their current circumstance. "But I've been in tons of relationships" seems to be the most common battle cry I hear among my circle. And sure, you probably were . . . in your twenties. In my twenties, I'd always have a boyfriend for about a year. Then they began to dwindle to six-month relationships, then three-month relationships, and finally just some dates here and there. Eventually, I just kind of felt like I was floating. I can't stomach the idea of being with someone just to avoid being alone, so I didn't force it with people I wasn't truly excited about.

There is one silver lining, though. Older single women may get written off as spinsters, witches, Forever-Alones, "too involved with animal rescue," or hot messes, but hey, at least they're not "creepy old men."

Aging single men aren't typically labeled lonely, pathetic, desperate, or sad—they get to be called "playboys," "ladies men," "hard to tie down," "the Dos Equis guy," or just sexy bachelors, like George Clooney (who eventually bit the bullet and got married; thank God Amal was smart and age appropriate!). But at a certain age, unattached men who are still pursuing much younger women start drifting into pervy territory. Don't believe me? Look at any woman's Instagram comments. Once an older male fan of mine didn't understand why writing, "I'd love to place a tender kiss on your perfect lips," was a creepy thing to do, which is the creepiest part! Point is, "creepy" isn't an adjective assigned to women unless they *really* try. As women age we might not be as sexually desirable, but we *are* still A-OK to hang out around kids, schools, and public parks!

Also, people don't generally attribute men's singleness to their being lame; they're single because no woman has been special enough to "tame" them. Newsflash: women do love a project, but no woman can change any man who doesn't want to change. Our Girl Logic kicks into overdrive when we encounter a mysterious, brooding hunk of dark, unpredictable moods. We become overwhelmed by his Potential, and we tell ourselves we're OBVIOUSLY the only woman alive special enough to coax him out of his shell. Because Girl Logic's dangling a carrot in front of us, making us think, "I'm special enough to change him," women put up with a lot.

And I do it, too. I do it with guys who aren't even real. I watch *Game of Thrones* and think, "Wow, Ramsay Bolton is cute and mysterious in a misunderstood, undiagnosed way. I know he loves torturing people, but I feel like he could change. If he got a chance at real love with someone like me, who knows what kind of adorable butterfly would flutter out of his hardened rapist shell!"

But think of all the free time women would have, all the mental energy they'd save, if they could turn off GL and stop constantly obsessing about being single! Men don't seek out relationships the way the majority of women do. Maybe it's a California thing, but I see guys every weekend "going surfing," "backpacking with the boys," or "staying in to unwind." Of course girls partake in leisure, too; it just feels like a lot of men are doing it to get away, while women are doing it to show off how much fun they're having on social media while obviously not thinking about boys at all.

There is a dusty, arid hole in the earth in Los Angeles called Runyon Canyon. Go there any day of the week, and you'll see anyone from celebrities to jeans-clad Estonian tourists hiking. It's dog friendly, which is great! Dogs love to pee there, and on a really hot day your hike is enhanced by the smell of warm dog urine baking in the sun. I went there alone for a few days in a row, and I did something a little weird: I simply listened to the snippets of conversations I heard as people passed me.

About 70 percent of the fifty-ish conversations I heard were women talking about men. Bits like "and his work has just been so crazy," "I don't wanna look crazy," "I can't keep texting him," "but we had so much fun," and of course the occasional positive tidbit, too. The point is, the primary subject of most women's conversations was . . . men. The other 25 percent? Women talking about other women, and mostly in a negative way: "I love her, but she tries wayyyy too hard." The other

5 percent was anything from politics to job complaints; I even heard one girl talking about how the secret to great skin is to not use water when washing your face. If anyone has any insight on this method, I'm all ears.

Of the men I spied on, less than 10 percent of their conversations were about women. The majority were about sports, apps, activities, movies—ya know, life stuff.

I did this survey because I wanted some empirical evidence that women are spending too much time talking about relationships while men are just out there, living life, failing to freak out about dying alone. (It's possible they are freaking out internally; I didn't probe that deeply.)

And as much as I hate this data, the fact is that men don't have to freak out because their biological clocks aren't ticking so loud. Men *don't* have to try, especially if they have table manners and a decent job. Age and beauty are fleeting, but money and power are, seemingly, forever. Don't tell that to the ancient Romans or anyone who has ever declared bankruptcy, though.

Sometimes our GL lets us relax into accepting our own singleness for a minute (because the alternative is too exhausting). We need some downtime to recuperate, chug some Gatorade, and take a breather before we get back out in the game. I've felt this way after a bunch of lame dates: "I don't want to text this new guy. I don't want to put on a strapless bra and talk with another stranger about my favorite movies while feigning interest in what part of Pittsburgh he's from." Nope, tonight I'm calling three friends. We're gonna drink expensive liquor at my house, take muscle relaxers because why not, maybe go to a bar for another round, come home, and order food. And I'm not gonna wear makeup. Except maybe a tiny amount of mascara . . . and concealer. And lip gloss. Who knows, I might meet my soulmate tonight.

8

Girl on Girl

In a perfect world, ALL WOMEN WOULD SUPPORT EACH OTHER, NO MATTER WHAT. But we're all human. We like some people, we loathe others, and we're "meh" on the rest. And none of us are immune to the idea that we're all somehow in competition for this thing called happiness.

I'll confess: sometimes, when I meet another woman who looks like "competition," I might catch my GL fussing, "What does *she* have that I don't? How can I get what she has? More coconut oil? Deeper breathing? What do *I* have that she doesn't? Is she funny? Can she fill out boy shorts?" I suspect this urge to compare ourselves is part of a survival instinct left over from when we all lived in huts. We've gone from "How did she find that fruit?" to "How did she get *that* job, and why is her skin so dewy? Where did she get all those promo codes on Instagram for highlighter kits?"

Then I remind myself, "I'm funny; I have that." And most of the time I just move on, because life is too short to obsessively compare. Plus, you know what feels better than enduring the endless mental loop of "Why her, why not me?," to simply compliment her and ask, "I'm so impressed, how did you get that ___?" It feels good to make someone else feel good, and, who knows, you might learn something, like, "Girl, I use BBQ sauce on my skin! Can you believe it?"

It's hard to stay above the fray, though, when you're a woman in a male-dominated industry. I read a lot of comedy interviews, and journalists always inquire about what various artists think of each other. When they ask male artists about each other, the reporters tend to do it from a good-natured place; they assume there's a mutual respect already there . . . because, well, they're men. But when they ask me about other women, it can feel like they're trying to start a fight, like they *want me* to bash the other comedian.

Goading me into turning on the other woman makes a journalist's job easier, and he can crank out a careless story about women hating each other. I get it. It's more fun to think we loathe each other. If we have beef, we might fight. And if we fight? Who knows, gentlemen, we might start clawing each other, and then ripping each others' shirts off, and then DUH, we all know the next step after that: A FULL-ON LESBIAN MAKEOUT SESSION FOR YOU TO WATCH!

Why do well-meaning women—women who know better, feminists even—feel the need to tear each other down? Frankly, I think it's because, no matter how much progress this society has made, there are *still* limited opportunities for women. Women are left desperately trying to reassure ourselves, whether it comes to men or money or kids or jobs, that "there's enough to go around." And sometimes there is. But sometimes there just isn't, and feeling starved for opportunity can make anyone a little competitive.

To me, one of the most powerful elements of feminism is the acknowledgment that women are multifaceted beings with the freedom to do, think, feel, and say what we wish. This includes getting to decide who I like and don't like, based on the criteria I choose. If you take anything away from my version of feminism, know this: Real feminists judge everyone based on their actions and character. They won't hold it against you that you are a woman, but they won't give you special treatment because of it either. That's the world I'd like to live in.

In my act, I've joked that women hate each other—even our closest friends. "OMG, Stacey's such a bitch. No, I love her, I do. I'm just saying." And I meant it when I said it in my twenties, when life was one big whirligig warpath of new experiences and none of us knew who we were or what we were doing. OH AWESOME! I CAN DRINK MYSELF SICK WHILE I LIVE WITH THREE OTHER GIRLS IN A TWO-BEDROOM RAILROAD APARTMENT AND SMOKE POT AND EAT MYSTERY THAI FOOD AT 4 A.M. AND STILL GET UP FOR MY CRAP DAY JOB AT 8 A.M. AND AT-TEMPT HORRIBLE SEX WITH MY NEIGHBOR WHO I SECRETLY REALLY LIKE WHILE I'M ALSO STILL

TALKING TO LIKE THREE OTHER GUYS! NO, HEELS
TOTALLY LOOK FINE WHEN THEY'RE ONE SIZE TOO
BIG; NO ONE WILL NOTICE! WHO CARES IF I GOT
WASTED AT A WORK PARTY AND CRIED IN THE
BATHROOM? OOPS, I THREW UP IN SOME DUDE'S
BED—IT'S COOL! LET'S ALL BAND TOGETHER AND
IGNORE THAT ONE FRIEND! I'M FUCKING SOMEONE
FROM MY JOB! WE IGNORE EACH OTHER MOST OF
THE TIME AND GET JEALOUS WHEN THE OTHER
ONE FLIRTS WITH SOMEONE ELSE! I'M GONNA
THROW A DINNER PARTY, HOPE YOU LIKE CHEX
MIX!

And . . . then you're thirty. Time flies. But in the thirtysomething era of newfound adulthood, jealousy and resentment can start cropping up more than ever, especially on the
romantic front. It's a struggle out there, as we've determined,
and it can feel harder and harder to meet smart, cool men the
older you get. This can trigger our GL to get panicky and hyper-
sensitive, even with girlfriends—"IS THERE ANY LEFT FOR
ME? WHEN WILL IT BE MY TURN?"—if we're still looking
for partners in our thirties and beyond.

For example, a few years ago, a childhood friend, Sarah, got
engaged. I was super excited for her. Sarah and I had known
each other since we were fourteen, and, as adults in Los Angeles, I'd twice attempted to set her up. The first time was with a
comic who turned out to be kinda gross. (But he always seemed
fine onstage!) The other was, uh, another comic—I need to expand my male friend network—who got her to blow him in the

car and then stopped at Subway before dropping her off. Not a red-letter day for either of them. Point is, I tried!

So Sarah got engaged and asked me to meet her fiancé. I did, and he seemed lovely. After dinner I texted her, "James is wonderful, I'm so happy for you. Let me know if he has any cool single friends ;)."

She texted back, "try match.com babe"—no caps, no punctuation, no emojis. I felt stung, and when I replied that I can't do Match because, well, I'm on TV sometimes and that would get weird, she wrote back, "Don't know what to tell you! XO."

I'd love to tell *you* that I didn't feel a little hurt after reading those texts. Not because she told me to try Match, but because she seemed so curt and unhelpful. Maybe I overreacted or misinterpreted; maybe other women would have blown it off as no big deal. But in that moment, my Girl Logic started spinning out—and as per usual, the first thing it told me was, "See? There is no one left in your friend network to meet; everyone else is taken! Hurry up before it's only you and a cockroach left in a bargain bin!"

When I considered how to reply, my GL gave me several options. The first was freak out and assume my friend secretly despised me. But, being raised as a lady, GL quickly reminded me that she probably didn't mean it the way it sounded; after all, it is a text, and they're often misinterpreted. Girl Logic also told me that this was my friend, and although she hurt my feelings, if I lost it on her now I'd just look like an asshole in a moment that was supposed to be joyful. But I'd been supportive; I'd even sat through a long dinner where all they did was kiss each other. It felt like because she'd found her own happiness, she had better things to do now than care about mine, even for a text or two.

It's reality: Your girlfriends love you. But when it comes to your romantic life, they are often too preoccupied with their own to think about helping you improve yours. It's a sad hidden truth of Girl Logic: while we rely so heavily on our friends, we also secretly compare ourselves to them and pity them, and some of us might bail or fade away altogether when our circumstances have shifted and we don't have as much space in our lives for them anymore.

Don't get me wrong; I understand the excitement and warm fuzzies that coincide with being in a new couple. I also get that the lives of your single friends can sometimes start to look just a tiny bit sadder when you've found love yourself. You sit at dinner clutching your new boyfriend's hand while your single friend talks about some lame date who kept bringing up how much he tipped the waiter while insisting his brand-new motorcycle jacket—the one that's so stiff it makes him look like he's peeking out of an S&M game of Whack-a-Mole—just needs "breaking in." And you look at your friend and listen to her horror stories and think to yourself, "Oh my God, I'm soooooo glad I'm in a relationship and am no longer relegated to that miserable dating prison." And you feel warm and safe. Then, one day? Maybe your relationship ends. BAM. You're back to being one of the inmates in gen pop, thinking, "How the fuck did I end up here again?" And you go crawling back to your girlfriends for protection, who almost always take you back, because they understand.

Women aren't entirely to blame for this hardwired sense of girl-on-girl competition. We were dealt a shit hand starting with Adam and Eve. Wait, we had Lilith, too! And she came BEFORE Adam and Eve! Lilith was created as Adam's equal, not sprouted from his rib like Eve, and she was expelled from the garden because she wouldn't be submissive to Adam. He banished her and made a 2.0 model he wanted to control—Eve.

Remember you were told Eve was made from Adam's rib? Guess what, a rib is a bone; a bone is a metaphor for a dick. The Bible wants you to know that Eve was made from Adam's dick *for* Adam's dick. That's right, she was made to serve him. Which is why when she decided to eat from the tree of knowledge and started having her own thoughts, she became the know-it-all who corrupted Adam because she made him eat the apple, and, to pay for that, women now have agonizing childbirth. That's how the Bible story goes, right? I chose to look at it like she was curious and didn't wanna chill in the garden where there was no Wi-Fi. So she got bored and said, "I want what I can't have; I'm a woman!" and ate the apple, which prompted her to be like, "Fuck yeah, I want more knowledge! How do cows work? What's air? Why aren't there any non-evil cable companies?" So God punished her for wanting to learn, and Adam was just a poor hot dummy who went along with it.

(Side note: The idea that clothes weren't even invented but still Adam and Eve were like, "Hey God, we're hiding from you because we're naked," *doesn't make sense.* Somehow, though, we ignore the stupidity of the story while retaining the assumption that women are evil temptresses, not ambitious creatures with a thirst for knowledge.)

Point is, from the get-go, it's been excruciatingly difficult for women to be strong and make our way in this world. We've had to fight hard for everything we've achieved. And sometimes we've had to fight each other. We're taught to do it, we're trained to do it, and our most reactive, base-level Girl Logic tells us we HAVE to do it to get what we want. It's GL—or sometimes just gut instinct—not to like a woman who feels like a threat; say, your boyfriend's Eva Mendes–lookalike new boss, or Sharon in marketing who nabbed that shiny award you were angling for, or your best friend's new sidekick who's suddenly stealing her away every other night for girls' nights out, and, when you say you don't like her, your friend says, "Really? Jamie has never said anything bad about you." And you're like, "EXACTLY! She doesn't even mention me! At least I have the decency to talk shit on her!" Cut to immediately feeling like judgmental garbage. So what if Jamie is a member of Soho House, I know a bar that has free popcorn!

I am here to tell you: You can't always heed your Girl Logic. Sure, it's just trying to protect you when it decides that Sharon is an underhanded asshole trying to steal your job. Though the irregular, sometimes-irrational headphone cord knots of GL might kick into freak-out mode and tell us other women are out to get us, it's on us to choose how to react—to take the high road and attempt to act from kindness instead of fear or pettiness.

When I finally left my twenties behind, I realized that women don't *have to* hate each other. To my credit, I have never disliked other women because they were beautiful. I have always been a neofeminist, meaning I have never blindly accepted a woman or anyone, simply because of her gender. If I don't like a woman, it is because she's shitty, not because of how she looked. I can't stand fake people, and if you suck, I can't sit through brunch with you. Any woman I might not have initially liked through ignorance, sense of perceived threat, or whatever, I have overcome by being nice to her and simply introducing myself. OK fine, if you're jealous of Scarlett Johansson and you try to conquer that by introducing yourself randomly to her at a Starbucks, her security might intervene. But, for me, when it comes to other comics, colleagues, or women at auditions, all it takes is a hello and sometimes a compliment. Remember, everyone wants to be liked! People respond kindly if you are kind. It really is that simple most of the time.

Of course, it's not like my female friendships are all rainbows and sunshine. Occasionally you'll have to confront a friend about saying something dumb, behaving weirdly, or just hurting your feelings. The important thing to remember, when your head is spinning in that kind of situation, is that when you speak from your highest self—from a perspective of truth and love—nothing bad can truly happen. When you confront a friend, if you approach it from a place like, "I want to let you know I am hurt, and I want to resolve it," your intentions are pure. Even if she reacts negatively, that's her deal—it's not on you. Instead of stewing and freaking out, you can use your Girl Logic to help you map out the best- and worst-case scenarios: "My friend cares about me, so she will want to fix this; we will both end up feeling totally fine about things again. If I bring this up and she shuts me down, oh well, worst case comes true, and she isn't my friend anymore, or we take a break to figure shit out and discuss it later." Either way, using your GL to help you plot the right course can help you avoid pitfalls, reduce anxiety, and do the right thing when it comes to dealing with hiccups in your relationships with other women.

As I've told you, building close female friendships hasn't always come easy for me. Because of that, I appreciate the girlfriends I have today even more. At this age, friendships aren't convenient. No, the stakes are high and life is hectic. If you don't have the scaffolding of school or work to support your friendship, and you still stay close? That means you really love each other. I remember visiting Calgary once, and I dropped into a club to do a guest set. I laid low in the back of the room, sort of keeping to myself. This woman came bouncing over to me. She was in her early forties and had huge hair. She giggled and said, "My name is Lori Gibbs, I'm a comedian here, and I want to be best friends with you." It was the beginning of my career, so I hadn't met many other women on the road, let alone women who were this pumped to meet me. We talked and talked and became friends. She's a comedian, housewife, mother of two, and she has a "Have Fun" tattoo on her forearm. I mean, who wouldn't want to be best friends with this woman?

That was over five years ago; now she features for me regularly, and I stay at her house whenever I go to Calgary. We spend our weekends together napping, crafting, and doing comedy. She feels like home when I'm far away.

Another time, a few years back, I was on the Comedy Store's patio, and a girl came up to me with her parents. It was sweet—they had been fans since I was on *Last Comic Standing,* and the girl was a comedian herself, a friend of a friend. She was cool, smart, funny, and just so charming. We became friends, and she decided to move to New York to do stand-up there. Our friendship morphed from a fan thing to a mutual respect, and now she features for me whenever I play the East Coast. Her name is Kate the Wasp, and she's awesome.

Do I befriend every woman or female comedian who talks to me? No. But I appreciate real women who aren't trying to get something out of me, who bring not just humor but hustle. These women were going to work hard with or without me, and I respected that. I'm glad they were willing to come up, say hi, and be vulnerable. It makes me more likely to be that way, too. It's also nice to be reminded that, in such a competitive industry, we truly can be friends.

Of course, I'm not some socially evolved feminist goddess who's risen above ever feeling threatened by another woman. Sure, I've matured, but I'm still a person. I'm still a girly-person! But I never wake up in the morning setting out to be any sort of monster, to other women or anyone else. (Okay, maybe I've fantasized about a few arguments, but they never come to fruition.)

But I like to think we all start our days with the best of intentions, with our Girl Logic leading us toward being bright, gleaming white lights of potential. Then our days roll on, and our GL might start growing muddier after we check Twitter and encounter sweet missives like "You're a dumb bitch and I hope your dog dies." While I know said assholes are losers with their accounts on private, sometimes I can't help but think to the universe, "Really? I haven't even opened my other eye yet and that's the first thing you throw at me?" Bright white light gets downgraded to an eggshell white. Or a beigey, coffee-stained white. Or a burned cream with blood spatters.

By the end of the day, after rejections, harassment, dropping your phone five times, watching the news, realizing your vote didn't count, breaking up, shitting your pants, whatever, your soul has morphed from luminescent light to a dull poop brown. By now your GL might be telling you to check the fuck out, curl up in a ball, and hide away from the world. At least until tomorrow. And you know what? Sometimes you *should* curl into a ball. Sometimes the energy of a day is so fucked, all you can do is go home, turn off your Twitter, sleep it off, and see what the lottery brings you tomorrow.

9

The Unfunny Chromosome

Women are so afraid of not being liked or, worse, being misunderstood, that we sometimes bite our tongues or don't act on our best impulses. Girl Logic is constantly assessing the ins and outs of every scenario from every angle, and it can become overly preoccupied with being liked; with perpetually maintaining the facade of the nice, good, sweet girl. For example, when a guy says something shitty to you out of nowhere, your Girl Logic might shut you up because you don't want to "cause drama," instead of knocking him out (a risky and potentially illegal move) or laying into him. As women, we don't have the luxury of saying, "Fuck it, here comes the BOOM," because of the magnified potential ramifications on every front: physically, emotionally, and professionally. And, sure, taking the high road is usually the right thing to do, but sometimes we want to fire off a warning shot; let someone know, "Hey, by the way, I could destroy you." We don't do it, though, because we see too many ways it could go wrong for us. (God, I wish I were less thoughtful. Sometimes I envy crazy people.)

What if someone in your office talks down to you? What if speaking up could affect your shot at a promotion? What if you're working at a comedy club and the emcee keeps demeaning you by calling you a "sexy funny lady" . . . to your own room full of fans? What about when you're going out and you don't feel like dressing up and you say, "Fuck it, I'm wearing overalls and dressing for me," and, oops, it turns out that was the *one time* you actually needed to care because all of your crushes from high school and the movies are in one bar!?

Girl Logic is about wanting to make yourself happy and make everyone else happy. And, sometimes, you end up making yourself unhappy because you're trying to make everyone happy. The truth is, the more successful you are, the more respected you are when you call the shots. That emcee who wouldn't stop bringing up my looks and gender? I told the club manager if he did it again, he would be fired. The guy was so scared that he not only gave me a sanitized intro, he didn't step foot in the green room the rest of the weekend. And do you know what gave me the confidence to request that I be treated professionally? I had sold out that weekend. I had money on my side.

Working as a comic has drilled this lesson into my being over and over again. It's invaluable, but it can hurt. To me, being a stand-up comedian is kind of like being an X-Man— you're born that way. From a young age, stand-up comedians have a natural proclivity for observation and introspection. But when I started out in stand-up, I knew *nothing* about show business. I had never heard of any club other than the Addison Improv, and that was because I passed it on my drive to high school every morning. I would always check the marquee to see who was there. What's so trippy to me, even to this day, is remembering names up there from when I was sixteen . . . and now those comics are my colleagues. Still blows my mind.

Because I was funny growing up, it never occurred to me that women *weren't* funny (or that other people might not recognize them as such). I was funny, Ellen was funny, Paula Poundstone was funny, all the *SNL* women and sitcom stars like Roseanne and Brett Butler were funny. It sucks, but women have to go above and beyond; be extra creative. Oh, you're in a sketch troupe playing the "ditzy southern girl" or the "hot dumb girlfriend" or the "mom"? What a creative character choice! But, for the longest time, those were all the options girls had. You almost had to earn your way up to the unique characters. You had to fight the typecasting and kick your way to the top to get to showcase a character like Mary Catherine Gallagher or Colette Reardon on *SNL*, or Megan Mullally as Karen on *Will and Grace,* or all of the women on *Golden Girls,* or anything Laurie Metcalf has ever done. You had to deal with years of twentysomething white guys getting the good lines in the sketches, and the good stand-up spots, and the immediate acceptance from the audience. As a woman, you had to *know* you had something special to create. What I didn't know before I started was that it would be such a fight. No one told me.

When I started out at twenty-two or so, I knew nothing but my jokes. I didn't know how agents worked, and I hadn't grown up studying stand-up. I just knew that there were people out there being funny for a living, and I was going to be one of them. I didn't have a concrete goal. The extent of my preparation for Hollywood was writing sketches for my friends, filming them in my living room, and then editing them on a Mini DV tape; God, I spent a fortune on those. In college at Emerson, I wrote and produced a ton of sketch comedy, and at the end of school I did a one-woman show. This is a right of passage for most creative women—venturing onto the stage alone, living and dying by your own comedy. It's a puddle of simultaneous giddiness, exhilaration, anxiety, and loneliness, and it's worth every well-timed minute.

Also, performing in a one-woman show during college is the only chance most women have to expose their breasts in the name of art. (I chose not to, but I would probably do it now! For the "likes.") See, college is a safe space for women to artistically explore their own sexuality—you're given free rein to dress provocatively, to turn on your audience, to use yourself as a character of sorts.

Tangential side note: in college ALL my acting friends wanted to be in a student film where there was a sex or rape scene. It's kinda funny and kinda disturbing, but honestly, who could blame them? "Art" is a perfect guise under which it's A-OK to explore the vulnerability of sexuality without being punished for it. And I was certainly not above attempting to be sexual on screen. Somewhere there exists footage of a fifteen-year-old me fake-crying in the shower after an off-camera rape scene. We shot it at camp. I was in a Tommy Hilfiger bathing suit. It was highly inappropriate for Summer Session I Video Production. Seventeen years later I ran into the kid who "directed" that film. I was drunk at 1 a.m. at South by Southwest and I said, "OH MY GOD YOU HAVE A TAPE OF ME AT FIFTEEN, HALF-NAKED AND FAKE-CRYING!" and without missing a beat, he said, "I KNOW! I CAN'T SHOW ANYONE OR I'LL GO TO JAIL!"

When I started out in 2005, doing stand-up about women's bizarre behaviors wasn't a "thing" like it is today. I was the only comedian getting up there as a young woman, and, without being overtly crass, talking honestly about the everyday girl experience: our behaviors, expectations, our desires, and our kooky inner monologues, everything from wedges to being obsessed with fall. I talked about Girl Logic. The constant barrage of information we would use to plan a night out: "Do we share tapas? Can we split a bottle? Should we text boys? Which boys? What if we text boys and only the ones we don't like show up? What if two we like show up? Should I bring a jacket? What if I have to carry it? What if I have to walk far and look cute? But what if I'm cold? Do I have cash for a cab? What if we want to eat late night? What if my shoes hurt my feet? Will I look weird if I wear flats?"

Soon, shows like *Girl Code,* a show that is just girls talking about being girls, appeared. Then there were the excessive numbers of mean-spirited, mocking Instagram accounts. If you haven't noticed, there are tons of accounts that exist for the sole

purpose of making fun of women's makeup, bodies, clothes, anything, and everything. One recent meme said something like,
"She doesn't do gluten, GMOs, or processed anything, but she
pops MDMA for two days straight at Coachella." As if there
aren't plenty of men out there with similar food restrictions who
drink to excess and do mountains of blow and HGH or, ew,
drink Gatorade with dinner. Where are the accounts picturing
some ugly bald dude, noting that he "can't talk to girls, is a little
racist, and is unhealthily close to his mom—but he made $5 mil-
lion last year with an app so he's allowed to be a monster"? And
the fact still remains that if and when there are memes making
fun of men, the impact isn't felt as fully for men as it is for
women, since women are already under constant attack. There
are thousands of accounts endlessly enforcing the idea that your
vagina has to be perfect, your body has to be flawless, and as long
as you're being "bae," you're cool. If these accounts are run by
men, or, worse, women, they're just feeding into our society's
desires to make women seem inherently awful. I'm not saying
that some of them aren't funny, what I'm saying is that shitting
on women is ubiquitous.

Anyway, back to stand-up. You don't have to be especially
tough to do it. Sure, it requires sufficient inner fortitude to deal
with rejection, but other than that you don't have to possess
much other than a strong sense of self and a burning desire to
share your observations with the world. I knew I was funny
because that was the staple compliment I'd received all my life.
Of course, I didn't know how many terrible guys I'd come up
against after I won *Last Comic Standing* in 2008. Since I had no

formal stand-up experience at that point, winning *LCS* was a little like trying to get into the military but skipping basic training and heading right to BUDS.

When I auditioned for *LCS* at twenty-five, I still had a day job in an office. I worked as an assistant at a company called the Ultimate Blackjack Tour—or the Ultimate BJ Tour, as I would call it when I instant-messaged my friends at work. I was the assistant to the head of marketing, and my duties included making copies, putting together press kits, and faking being awake at 10 a.m. when I was hungover. I would pull up a Word doc, prop up my head to look like I was reading, and . . . fall asleep. I had a passion for neither blackjack nor marketing, but it was a good gig; I was proud to have my own cubicle! I remember the day I got offered the job. I called my mom and screamed "I'm making $40K A YEAR!" To the twenty-four-year-old me, new to the corporate world, it might as well have been a million dollars.

I didn't even know what the prize for winning that damn reality show was. I had no real outside guidance or even a personal objective. I just knew it would be a good thing if more people could see me doing stand-up. Getting on *Last Comic Standing* equaled validation.

I missed the LA audition because I was in Singapore doing military shows. I flew to San Francisco to audition, did my joke, and got through. That joke may or may not have been about pizza—that is, how shitty pizza places always sell you "'three pizzas for fifteen dollars with free cheesy bread and marinara dipping sauce!!!' I'm like, cheesy bread with marinara sauce?

Uhhh, that's the same as pizza!" Anyway, I was asked to come back that afternoon for the taped auditions. The rest is history.

I'm only telling you this story about my first break because I want to reveal the realities behind, well, reality shows. At least, *my* experience with them. I went through what should have been a unique, fun, formative Hollywood experience. I'm a woman, though, and women have to work ten times as hard just to wait for the audience to recover from the fact that we aren't men. So instead of being something inspiring and awesome, my experience on *LCS* turned out to be a mentally scarring emotional gauntlet.

One component of my season was that the last batch of remaining comics were all sent to live in a house together, have their lives taped, and see what happened when people stopped being polite . . . and started getting real. JK that's a different (but kinda the same!?) show. But, really, we did go live in a house together. I'd seen enough reality shows to know that the sole purpose is pitting them against each other to try to eke out twenty-two minutes of fantastic TV.

I wasn't loud, confrontational, or combative, not in the house or in real life. I didn't try to be funny, or hypersexual, or "the bitch," even though I knew they needed a bad guy and I'd heard they were out to make "the blonde girl from Dallas" look like one. So I decided from day one that they would never get anything out of me other than smiles—certainly nothing negative about any other contestant. I focused entirely on why I was there, which involved some strategy. It was 2008, the prime of reality TV, and I watched it all: *Flavor of Love, Rock of Love,*

Flavor of Rock. I learned two things from these shows. One was how to physically assault another woman you just had a filthy drunken three-way kiss with. The other was in the editing. When the producer sits you down for an OTF (on-the-fly interview), they like to interrogate you about the other cast members. And the second you mention another cast member, the show cuts to footage of *them.* I'd worked very hard to stay in that house, so I rarely, if ever, said anyone else's name. I tried to talk only about my own comedy. Hey, I knew what an amazing opportunity I'd been given—I wasn't going to give up my screen time to someone else!

I also paid attention to story editing. When you watch a reality show, producers sometimes invent their own creative story-line for each cast member. They can create villains and heroes, editing it however they want to bend reality to their perceptions. You can say something as simple as "I love Steve! Last night Steve made me dinner and afterward I was so so full I almost died." But that sweet, positive sentiment can quickly translate to, "Last night Steve made me dinner [*insert shot of Steve smiling and cooking*]. . . . And I almost died" [*insert shot of you full on the couch but not smiling*]. All of a sudden, Steve has gone from someone you adore who cooked you an amazing dinner to someone who tried to poison you. Now America hates Steve.

At the end of each week, the members of the house got together and put in a vote for who they thought they were funnier than (brutal). After that, the person we said we were funnier than got voted off—but not before having the chance to "challenge" two other comics. Then the THREE of you had to perform in front of a live crowd, which ultimately decided who got to stay. So while I was never weak enough to be voted off, two weeks in a row I was viewed as weak enough to be challenged by the loser who was being kicked off. And each week, I won.

And that's why I won the show. Because, despite proving myself week after week, day after day, the guys *still* assumed that challenging the girl was their best shot at staying. I used my GL for one element of this: I weighed how easy it would be for them to grab a sound bite and make me look like a bitch. I wanted to be liked because of me. I didn't want to be disliked because of something some producer made me up to be. People expect women to be weak, bitchy, and easily defeated, and I made sure to let them down.

GL will sometimes kick in to remind you how things might go awry if you upset people or seem less than likeable, but I tried to remain calm and steady, knowing one wrong move could turn into producers portraying me as the SuperBitch. I moved forward, questioned nothing, and did what I had to do. When it came time for America to vote on who would ultimately get voted off each week, our fair country had already gotten to know me. I was the underdog who wouldn't quit, and they liked that. I won by a landslide.

Did I deserve it more than the other guys? In that pantheon, yes. In life? Who the hell knows. But I know I didn't deserve it *less* than they did. I worked my ass off to be there. Now, there's no such thing as "deserve" when it comes to art.

The same rule that allows a three-year-in comic to win a national TV show is the same rule that applies when you've made four pilots that never got picked up. It isn't fair, and you never know what could happen down the road. We sign up for that chaos as entertainers.

After I won the show, though, things took a decided turn for the worse. At least when it came to the way my male castmates treated me. Fragile egos, I suppose. I'm not using names here because it's not my intention to be a shit-talker. But, during the course of the season, I'd befriended a hilarious guy in the house; let's call him Dave. We were good friends, and we spent our nights in the kitchen of that comedy house talking about comedy and movies. We both had significant others, so it was nice to just bond as colleagues and castmates. On the night of the finale, NBC threw a party. I spotted Dave, and I was so excited to introduce him to Andriana, my Semester at Sea friend, who had flown out to Vegas for the finale. But, when I tapped him on the shoulder and he turned around, I swear his eyes looked pitch black—soulless and empty. He simply said, "You shouldn't have won. I should have. Good luck following me for the next four months," and stormed off. I was floored. I had never had anyone turn on me like that.

After the show, me and the four dudes I beat got to do a cross-country tour together. Wahoo! That was the beginning of four months of misery; day-in, day-out mental abuse. Apparently Dave had poisoned the other comics against me, and I had to sit idly by as they all, one by one, quietly stopped talking to me. No one would save me a seat at dinner, no one would sit by me on the bus, no one would say "bless you" if I sneezed, nobody would answer if I asked a question, and no one would *ever* laugh if I made a joke. Not knowing if you're gonna be met with hostility, warmth, or just be totally ignored anytime you speak is maddening. This was my introduction to the world of professional stand-up as a ruthless, bitter, competitive wonderland where people are jealous of you for being what they aren't and despise you for being what you are.

But what was I gonna do? Not headline the tour I had earned? No way would I quit, and I certainly wouldn't give them the satisfaction of crying in front of them. So I decided to keep getting on the tour bus every week and let them be pieces of shit while I sat quietly on my own and . . . endured.

Every day was me putting on a brave face and putting my energy into the set I'd scraped together to headline the tour. Dave would often go right before me and would do his best to bury me at every show. And he was SO funny; I have no problem admitting that. Sure, there were shows in which he may have performed better than me, but that didn't change the fact that I was being paid more. I'd won the show—people were coming to see me, and I'm sure that killed him.

All I did to deserve these men's mistreatment was refuse to roll over when they knocked me down. And I know I'm not alone in dealing with this sort of thing from colleagues. It happens all the time; welcome to womanhood, right? Because you're not willing to disappear or take it, because you just want the respect everyone else seems to command simply because they're bestowed with a dick, you get labeled bitchy, or "difficult."

To make it worse, we also had to do press. Photo ops, newspaper interviews, radio tours, all as one supposedly big happy comedy family. And of course all the journalists would ask, "So how's the tour going?" For the sake of the show, I lied, smiled through gritted teeth, and claimed we were having "so much fun." Ugh.

Then one night, one of them called me a cunt.

"Robert," one of the comics I had become sort of friendly with, seemed gentle before all this. While Dave had strived to make my life miserable at every turn, Robert, it seemed, was unaffected at the beginning. He was indifferent to me, and I took that nugget of apathy as a port in the storm. We'd even gotten pedicures together in one city at the start of the tour. I felt, if nothing else, we had at least become friendly. One night, we were getting drinks at a bar after a show. I guess Robert is a nasty drunk? Or something? Because out of nowhere he let loose this zinger: "You think you're so much better than all of us!"

As a comedian, there is that split second when someone says something insane that you think they must be joking because, had you said something like that, you know you'd be joking. But he wasn't. My stomach dropped. This kind of accusation was uncharted territory for me. I also didn't think that at all. Now, now I do. But I didn't then.

"And you didn't deserve to win. You are a fucking cunt." The other comics just stood next to him, emotionless, as if he had uttered something as banal as "I'm gonna go find the buffet."

I turned around and walked away as fast as I could to my hotel room, where I finally broke down crying. Not because he called me a cunt—but because it felt like he had been saving up the word for weeks, just to spit it out at me whenever he was ready. We had just gotten pedicures! I felt safe with him! He at least had to have a mother!? Yet, to him, I wasn't a normal woman or human; I was just some horrific bitch who had stolen his last chance at a career and thus didn't deserve . . . anything.

Needless to say, the next few tour stops were pretty much the opposite of fun. And I realized that I was protecting the *Last Comic Standing* brand—a brand that ultimately didn't care about me. (Have you seen me on the show since?) At the same time, I was protecting a bunch of dick comics who seemed to find joy in trampling on my emotions on a daily basis. Exhausted, I gave an interview to a small paper in Florida and admitted that the guys weren't, and I'm paraphrasing here, "that cool to me." I put it mildly; I had no desire to embarrass anyone. Of course the guys all had Google Alerts on their names, and the next morning on the bus, Robert stormed at me with a printed copy of the interview, smoke coming out of his ears.

"LOOK WHAT *SHE* SAID ABOUT US!" he shrieked, his battle cry to rally the others. Apparently this pathetic one-line statement from me was enough probable cause for them to let loose on me. And finally, finally, I snapped and gave it right back to them: "YOU MOTHERFUCKERS ARE LUCKY THAT'S ALL I SAID! I'VE BEEN FUCKING PROTECTING YOU THIS WHOLE TIME!" I yelled. Robert threatened to hit me; he literally said, "I should punch you in the face!" What's funny is, in the moment, I didn't feel threatened as much as sorry for him, sorry for him that this is what his life had amounted to, threatening me with physical violence. The tough guy in me chuckled a little like, "Oh my God, hit me and watch what happens. Watch how your life unravels when people find out you hit a twenty-five-year-old woman." No one hit me.

But the screaming fits just escalated all around. Have you ever screamed at someone you weren't prepared to scream at? I could almost feel myself leaving my body as a cold sweat covered me and my voice shook from surprise, uncertainty, and this weird sense of knowing, deep down, that these fuckers had it coming. Still, I couldn't believe this explosion was happening.

When the tour finally wrapped up after a few months, I was left hardened, emotionally, and really thin, physically. I remember my manager asking, "Why are you so skinny?" And I said, "I sleep all day because I'm anxious about the guys, and I eat one meal alone at the theater."

What I gained from the whole nasty debacle—um, in addition to a new fan base, of course—was an incredibly thick skin. Most likely, nothing I'll ever endure in show business will be worse than *that*. The whole experience lit a fire under me to never be a victim like that again, to never just take shit because someone thinks I don't deserve what I have. Now I'm a little like your grandpa; you know, the one who has been in combat and seen some shit. Once you've seen the worst, nothing fazes you. I can honestly say I'm not afraid of any experience . . . at least not in show business. Real life is still a terrifying mystery, as are white jeans.

Before that experience, I worked hard. I would do my job from 8 a.m. to 6 p.m., and then I would find dinner and hit the town to do my spots. Five minutes at the Store, ten minutes on the West Side. One time I drove to San Diego and back on a work night because they gave me twenty minutes. I hustled. I produced comedy shows, I wrote sketches for people, I got stage time anywhere I could. I had energy and I used every ounce of it. Work ethic is something you can learn, and, in some cases, it's in your DNA.

My parents divorced when I was seven, remember? Recently my father and I got in an argument. When parents divorce there's always a gray area regarding which parent did the most, tried the hardest, all that. In the heat of our argument, I said something about my father not being there enough. He replied, "You have no idea how much I wanted to be with you. I had to be on the road five days a week, and I would drive all night long on Friday, chugging coffee and listening to the Mets game to stay awake. All so I could be there to make breakfast for you and your brother on Saturday morning." I learned two things from that! The first was the origin of my road-dog work ethic, and the second was that hard work and intention often go unnoticed. All people see is what you *don't* do or what they think you should be doing better.

There was a comic, years ago, who was younger than me (he still is). Over the course of a few weeks, I would regularly drop into the Comedy Store to refine a routine I was working on for TV. I just needed five minutes to try out some of the material. One of the benefits of being a paid regular is that you can drop in during a certain time and just get on stage for a couple minutes, run a few jokes by the tourists to see what's funny. So I popped in, and the emcee told me he'd put me up next. The younger comic approached me: "Hey Iliza, I feel like every time you come in, you bump me; is it cool if I just do my set? I was next."

My Girl Logic whispered, "You aren't trying to be rude, and if he thinks you are deliberately trying to be rude, he will tell other guys and they will all dislike you. If he gets a show, he won't want you on it. He could become King of Comedy, and you'll be left in the dust. So try not to upset him." Then another part of my brain, a newly built defensive side, screamed over my GL, "IT'S ANOTHER *LAST COMIC STANDING*! DON'T LET HIM TAKE WHAT'S YOURS! HOW DARE HE MAKE THIS PERSONAL AND QUESTION YOU!" See, often my GL, in the name of self-preservation, has me map out arguments for bad news I haven't even received yet—bad news I actually might never receive. I plan it out so that if and when something awful I imagined actually happens, I have a "choose your own adventure" response instantly at the ready.

But when he asked me that question, I was caught off guard, so I temporarily ignored my GL and just said, "OK." After all, it was only five minutes, and it seemed to mean something to him. Of course my objective in stopping in there wasn't to bump him in particular, but . . . that's comedy. People get bumped. Chris Rock can come into any club, and the whole lineup falls by the wayside if he wants to do time. I couldn't help but feel that he wouldn't have been as vocal if a successful male comic had dropped in.

So, after the show, I called him. I couldn't stomach the thought of (A) him thinking I was out to get him and (B) him thinking it was OK to just walk up to a woman who outranked him and ask her to, like, chill.

When he picked up the phone, I let my GL dictate the first sentiment of my call: "I just wanted to let you know that, when I drop in, I'm only there to work on my set. I don't know who's before or after me, and I don't want you to think I'm targeting you. I'm not." Then . . . I let my ego do the rest of the talking! "But please don't tell me not to bump you, you don't get to do that. Just like I wouldn't tell Adam Sandler not to bump me. It's part of the game, and it isn't personal. You don't have the right to say that to me, I've been at this longer, and I have more credits."

I didn't whine, I didn't sugarcoat it. I spoke to him like a man. And he got it. Whether he acquiesced out of astonishment, fear, respect—I didn't care. But I haven't had a problem with him since, and now we always say hi to each other.

See, you teach people how to treat you. If you don't like someone's behavior toward you, educate them. Your Girl Logic might be urging you to crawl into a corner, to cry or sulk and pretend it's not happening. And of course you need to pick your battles: we can't flip our shit every time a man addresses us a little oddly. (And you might not want to! You don't have to rabble-rouse for gender equality every single time a man calls you "sweetie.") But if you aren't getting the respect you deserve, demand it . . . or ignore that person for the rest of your life. OR go out and make your career infinitely better than all those motherfuckers combined. Any of those options should work.

10

It's All About the "At Bats"

When it comes to pursuing your passions in life, the stakes are always higher for women. When we have the audacity to pour ourselves wholly into a goal, it can . . . kinda scare people. And the more passionate you are about what you want, the louder GL will be ringing in your head, especially when you get pushback from a world that says you're too fat, not pretty enough, too loud, overly aggressive, whatever. But as it is with so many other areas of life, Girl Logic can be both a boost *and* a bummer in this realm. It can lay out all the ways you can fail—fired, not enough views of your videos, producer doesn't watch your tape—*and* how you might feel afterward, since failure is part of your rich history as a human who gives a damn. And it can also remind you that there is absolutely no downside to trying. So you try and fail, so what? You did your best, you still got the lessons. Plus, the more you fail, the less it hurts.

My whole life, my stepdad has described chances as "at bats"—meaning how many times you're allowed to step up to the plate and swing, hit or miss. You get "at bats" because you're good enough to miss and still be invited to the plate. Though I always strive to succeed (who doesn't?), I'm *allowed* to fail, to have "at bats," because I work hard to earn them. Where others give up, I press on. Where others are complacent, I push. I don't do it for any reason other than it's the only way I know how to be.

I believe my work ethic was passed on to me by my father. While I have the utmost respect for my mom, who was a working single mom when she raised me, I connect with my father more when it comes to professional ambition. For twenty-seven years, my father worked in men's apparel—things like ties, suspenders, and belts. He spent twenty-seven years on the road as a sales rep, driving all over the country every week. Now, when I'm touring, I'll get calls from my dad on a Sunday: "I figured if it's Sunday, you're in an airport flying home." And we'll talk about the city I was just in. He knows all of them, down to a detail like, "On Third and Washington, there's a restaurant that makes a clam pizza. It sounds disgusting, but trust me, it's unfuckingbelieveable."

My working knowledge of most US cities consists of the immediate area around my hotel and the venue, but my father knows so many cities intimately from pushing giant rolling racks up and down streets, from store to store. After years and years of working for someone else, he started his own line of apparel; named it Novia. I would go visit him in the summers in his office/warehouse. He would let me cut swatches of silk and glue them to expensive card stock as samples for customers. I wasn't great at it, but who is? It's actually really hard to freehand-cut a perfect square with pinking shears!

I remember going to the factories where they would cut leather and dye alligator pelts that would be later made into belts and braces. I'd crawl past the machines and under the cutting tables to collect the leather scraps, positive I could create something special with the shreds of discarded materials. I couldn't.

My father did everything himself, putting everything he had into that business. He ran the warehouse, designed the merchandise, boxed it up, and sold it. He would go, store to store, meeting to meeting, state to state, to sell them on the idea of carrying his line. He would fly to Lake Como, Italy, to the silk mills, to design the patterns for his ties. What a schlep. We couldn't go to a mall without my dad stopping into a few stores just to see who carried what; he was *always* doing research.

To this day, my father still points at stores we drive by and declares, "I used to sell to them."

I do the same thing when I pass a random building I once worked at in Los Angeles. I can't help but point it out to whoever I'm with: "I did a show there once." No one cares but me, but it's a funny thing to measure a lifetime of accomplishment by staring at buildings you once worked in. I imagine myself, old and gray, telling my grandkids, "I once did a show for five people in the upstairs of an Acapulco Mexican restaurant! Now it's a robot grocery store!"

I guess I never assumed the business wasn't doing well because he was my Dad and he worked hard.

Slowly, the menswear business dried up. Sure, men still needed accessories, but the market grew smaller and more competitive. I was twenty-one and home from college, about to make my move to Los Angeles. I was in the car with my father. I thought he was just dropping me off, but he put the car in park. He looked at me and, with tears in his eyes, explained how difficult it had been for him, closing his business and having a family to support. He knew giving up wasn't an option, and he wanted me to be proud of him. *Me* proud of *him*? The thought had never occurred to me. Parents are supposed to be proud of their kids, right? The other way around seemed, well, irrelevant; why would an adult care what a kid thought?

As an adult, I understand what losing a business must have been like for him. It's like losing a part of your soul. It's an entity you've poured your sweat and tears into; it reflects you, and when it dies, you lose something major. It's a little like a breakup, or even a death. You wonder what more you could have done to save it, to turn things around. It's a part of your energy and life that is gone.

I remember crying for the whole weekend when my first late-night pilot didn't go through. I didn't understand how something I worked so hard for, something that had so much of my heart in it, could just be casually passed on. You can't help but wonder, "Was I not enough? Does the universe not want me to have what I want?" Or worse, "Am I as misguided as the 99 percent of delusional people out in Los Angeles—am I one of the crazies?"

No, the universe always wants you to be happy. And, in hindsight, that pilot was terrible. We'll blame the executives on that one, though. They wanted me to say stuff like "keep it 100!" Puke.

Anyway, I don't know if I had ever seen my dad cry, and he wasn't like, sobbing, but his eyes got that clear color that blue eyes get when holding tension and tears back. I know this look because I have his eye color and I happen to think I look really pretty when I cry. My dad explained that he was getting into a brand-new business: financial planning. Now, if that doesn't sound like a total Dad job, I don't know what does! But, beyond the job, what he was telling me was that he was starting over at forty-nine. At forty-nine with two children, a wife, a dog, a house—all the typical American Dream stuff surrounded by a nightmare of a situation. Here he was, at an age many men are starting to fantasize about retiring, in the process of completing the three exams necessary to acquire a license to practice a business he had never worked a day in. I was in awe of his fortitude. I think a change like that might paralyze some people, but he moved through it, with muscle and determination. Twelve years later, my father now teaches financial planning workshops and is one of the top financial advisors in his company. On that day, in that car, sitting in the sweltering Texas heat, my dad, through his actions, made it clear to me that nothing ever needed to stop me from moving forward with passion and purpose. Giving up is just not an option.

But that doesn't mean I don't struggle with the sting of failure or self-doubt. Here's an example of my GL-driven thought process on most things related to work. I get a call from my manager telling me, "The network wants to talk about your script." Because I've never had a script green-lighted before, my automatic defense thinking is, "Great, they're gonna pass on it." Then, feeling preemptively defeated, I start reevaluating all my other projects: "That won't go, and the other project won't go. And if that other thing doesn't go. . . . After a year and a half of writing, now I'm back to just doing stand-up? Fuck, I'm a total loser. I'm gonna be forty-three and playing a Giggle Shack in Dayton."

Then I'll sit with that. Maybe all day, maybe all week. In a way I guess I choose to focus on the negative versus basking in the positive; I use it as a motivation tool, but I also do it because some part of me doesn't think anything I've done is actually all that great. And I hate myself for it. It's hard wanting to move the cultural needle, be part of a bigger conversation, make an impact, but feel like I'm continually getting left out of bigger projects. I've never made a legit "top comics to watch" list. I've never been on any sort of tastemaker list. I don't have a ton of social media followers compared to most celebrities. I'm not part of anyone's passion project. I've never been on a hit TV show or really been in movies. Basically, for the past eight years, I've solely been doing stand-up, my failed pilots and auditions all relegated to my memory. And I love stand-up, so so much. But watching other people skyrocket past you—and this can obviously apply to many industries and various aspects of life—is, well, painful. This might read as sour grapes, but it isn't. I'm just being honest. It is possible to be happy and angry and proud and unsatisfied at the same time. That's not even Girl Logic, that's just a human experience.

Ever since I was a kid, I've been a questioner. While almost everyone else around me seemed to plod along buying into everything they were told, I was interrogating everything. "What do I really want? What's the point of all this? Why do I have to listen to what these idiots say? Why do I have to accept this ref's call in this game? Why do I have to say 'yes ma'am' to a teacher whose only intellectual saving grace is that she has an answer book?" A majority of people don't question anything ever. People too often think the hand they've been dealt can't be shuffled and redealt. There's just no way you don't possess the power to change your own reality. I'm not talking about in a metaphysical way; I have no idea how to explain that. I'm saying, whatever you want to do, there is no rule saying you can't. You want to be a comedian? Go to a local bar and ask if you can start a comedy night. Practice and carve out a path, whether it's classes, clubs, whatever. You want to be a scientist? Get up in that science! You got rejected from school? Good thing there are other schools out there. Remember, there's no reason you have to accept defeat. Don't believe me? Ask any immigrant living in America.

My cousin posted this meme once on Facebook: "Everyone is doing the best they can." And I did not "like" it, because I don't know if I truly believe that. People are doing what they can to get by, sure. But very few people are imbued with a passion, and where there is no passion, there is no concerted effort. Can you grow a passion if you don't have an innate one? Of course. You can call 1-800-Rent-a-Passion. No, but really—you may not know you have a proclivity for something until you're exposed to it, or thrust into it, or suddenly your life takes an unexpected turn, and that Thing is suddenly all you can focus on. Like those newspaper stories about the mom of a murder victim who becomes obsessed with getting a law degree and changing the system from the inside. She found her passion in a tragic way, but her life has meaning now.

I mean, even drug abuse gives people a passion! It's one of the few fucked-up paths you can go down where, if you survive it, you can turn around and educate others on the perils of addiction. I'm like, let me get this straight—so I didn't do drugs, didn't go to jail, and didn't accidentally kill someone with my car, but now YOU'RE the one with the twenty-four-college-a-year speaking-engagement schedule? Not fair.

Passion is doing something over and over and never growing tired of it. And no, breathing doesn't count. Anyway, I didn't know I would have a passion for stand-up comedy until I found myself obsessed with working at it, perfecting it. Everything from traveling constantly, to insisting on working while I'm sick, to seeing how many projects I can keep in the air at once; I have a passion for being as busy as I can be. But . . . only with comedy. I find a sick thrill in being overworked, in taking five meetings in a day and still having time to do three spots a night, as if someone is going to spontaneously hand me an award for Most Overextended at the End of the Year with, Like, an OK Amount of Results to Show for It. I also didn't know I had a passion for singing five-second songs to my dog on Snapchat until I started doing it. "Small and rare, small and rare. You shake it for cash, you do it for tips. Small and rare." is one classic. Another is "Tiniest woman in the world! Littlest doggy in the land! Tiny tiny tiny tiny tiny!" and "Ya gotta big butt and it's not your fault, ya gotta big butt and it's all your fault." These are the songs, along with about fifty others, that are on a constant loop in my brain.

And I didn't know I had such a passion for connecting with humans until my fans showed me how much my stand-up meant to them; now that connection is what drives me. Thanks guys.

What if you're someone who doesn't have a passion yet? I don't think you can force it, but you can hope for it, try new things, and keep striving for one. (And in my opinion, women are more adept at this than men are. Remember that part from the beginning of the book about women accumulating more and more hobbies and interests as they age? It's because our GL *wants* us to keep pushing and exploring. Our GL won't let us rest until we've found our true happiness, or at least pinned down a path toward it, because, again, we were told we could have it all.) Plus, I'd like to think everyone has something they have the potential to be both great at and greatly excited about. I would like to think that it's laziness that keeps people from being great, not ineptitude. Someone's gotta do the grunt work.

The majority of people out there have good hearts. But so many seem to simply be doing whatever they can to get by instead of pushing themselves to find a bigger meaning, which I realize isn't always easy, especially if you're born into shitty circumstances. You can be born rich, and having that inherent safety net makes you feel like you never need to strive for anything so you fuck around and maybe start DJing. You can be poor, and, well, you don't need me to explain why being poor presents major disadvantages all around. But I truly believe that caring about something (something besides, like, killing people) is the key to a fulfilled life. I'm fortunate to have found my passion from a young age. It's never occurred to me that I shouldn't be pursuing that, full speed ahead.

But as much as Girl Logic is trying to help us advance toward our true purpose, it can also be a burden. The fears start to swirl—go for your passion too hard and you might miss out on marriage. Travel the world and live free, well, you might miss out on a chance for a baby. Don't travel or wander enough, and you might miss out on, um, everything else.

We still keep trying to meet everyone else's ideals, but it's tiring. The year I wrote this book, 2016, was the culmination of years of hard work for me. I got a script into a network that had been in the works for two years. I created *Confirmed Kills* as my opus. I finally got a shot at a late-night show. But learning to let go of what others *think* I should be doing has been a long, tough process. And, fuck no, I'm not some Zen master who has magically learned to accept everything and everyone as they are. Dear God, sometimes it's so bad that I'll forget why I dislike someone and just hold onto the anger. All I'm left with is a vague, shapeless feeling of dissatisfaction cloaking my brain; it's like anger dementia. You'll go to hug me at a party, and after I flinch you'll secretly wonder, "What the hell did I ever do to her?" And I skulk away like, "You know what you did." But I don't even know!

Anyway, like I said—I realize I'm too tough sometimes.

I sat with that realization for a while after receiving one particular dressing-down. The gist of it was this: I had a show with a network, and execs pitched various ideas to me about how we might promote it. Of course, every idea was, well, epically wrong for me. They kept trying to shove me into some hypersexualized "sassy single girl" archetype, the one who constantly brags about one-night stands, the perils of dating, how hilariously pathetic my Saturday nights are, and why wine is my best friend. I'm not that girl, though. This happens a lot, of course; it's how you end up perched on a motorcycle in a leather jacket and too much black eyeliner thinking, "I took a boxing class, but I'm not *this* bad-ass. This feels off brand."

I made the mistake of expressing my displeasure. I can't remember whether I said I was offended (God forbid a woman be upset about your ill-conceived presumptions of her sexuality) or that I straight up didn't like their pitch. But months later, after a decent season, we were told that my show wasn't being renewed. Fine, whatever. That happens. Then it came down the pipeline that I was "difficult to work with."

What hurt wasn't that it got canceled, it was that one conversation, months ago, rendered me the scapegoat simply for standing up for myself. I might be particular, but I pride myself on being consistently on my game when it comes to work. I don't fuck around, show up late, or arrive not knowing my lines; I show up, do my job well, and leave. So, after that experience, I found myself feeling angry, sure. Unheard, yes. And . . . exhausted. I was angry that people can create art only to have faceless egg avatars shit on them. I was angry that women can work their whole lives only to be reduced to a Reddit thread about their tits. And I was angry that some executive took umbrage with my taking umbrage, and, rather than do his job and come up with a more creative idea, he took the lazy route and blamed me.

That's when I stopped giving a fuck about picking every battle (more on this to come shortly). I think there is a way to not care while still caring, if that makes sense. In the future I'll be more careful about who I say what to. Your GL might tell you to stand up for yourself, but it also reminds you that if you do, you run the risk of pissing off someone weaker than you—who might also be in a greater position of power. It's a tough call, and you can drive yourself mad weighing out all the outcomes. And, once in a while, you pick the right battle and you win.

My rule, in both work and life, is to always bet on myself—to stand up for myself to try to get a head start on all the haters. Jesus, I can't believe I sincerely used the word "haters"—may as well write the rest of the book as a SnapChat story.

Always do things your way first. If you have an idea for a project, lay it out there. If you love someone, say it. If you want something, fucking go for it. Hey, even if you fail, you'll know you gave it your all; it's hard to look back with regret on anything if you tried as hard as you could. Also? If it's your passion, you'll never actually give up. You might get tired, but you'll snap back.

About two years ago, I got in bed with A Very Good Production, Ellen DeGeneres's company. What I wanted to do was pitch a show about me and my life as a comedian. Which made sense; I mean, every meeting I took for the past three years, all anyone has ever talked about has been "women in comedy," "funny women," blah blah. I figured if Seinfeld, John Mulaney, Louie, and a smattering of other guys had gotten to write a show and proudly and openly proclaim that they were real-life stand-up comedians at the same time, who better than me to say, "I'm a woman and a stand-up, and this is my story"?

Ellen's company liked the idea, and they said I should get paired with a writer to draft an outline. At that time I had written one other script with *Sex and the City*'s Cindy Chupak. So the idea of being paired with a powerful, more seasoned writer seemed like the logical way to go. After all, I wasn't a sitcom writer.

A few weeks later I got a call telling me that this "acclaimed" writing team was interested in me. Knowing that I don't know everything, I met with them and signed on. Did I love them? Meh. But when the bigger picture is getting a show on a network, I decided I could learn to like them, especially if I had to learn that lesson from atop a pile of money.

Then . . . I got another call. They didn't like the comedian idea. Now they wanted to do a show about me and my dating life. I hated their take on it, and I asked if I could at least say I was a stand-up, so we'd each get something. They said I could mention it, but it was really about dating. OK, deep breath and repress the rage at being pigeonholed. Eye on the prize. We took some meetings and they wrote an outline.

For those of you who don't know, in Hollywood there's this time called "pitch season," when writers, comedians, and producers go to the networks to pitch ideas for a script.

A week before we were set to pitch the dating idea, the writing team called Ellen's production company: "We want full creative control." Since there were two of them, they already had 50 percent control. This wasn't a decision they were making after mulling it over; this was a strategic move, done at the last minute, to put pressure on me to say, "Oh no! I don't want to miss pitch season! Yes! You can have control, just get me my show!"

It didn't feel right. Creatively, emotionally, and ethically. So I said, "The idea that after this many years of me writing my own stand-up, that these two think they could write *my* voice and that I wouldn't be at every meeting and in every writer's room for this show is insane. They can't have full creative control. The answer is no."

They thought I was nobody, so they could bully me. Their people called back and said they weren't budging. I was faced with the idea of being underestimated and having to compromise myself creatively. I'm never opposed to taking advice and guidance from someone smarter; I'm always into the idea of collaborating with someone better than me. But I didn't know these people, and, well, they were assholes.

I called my agent back and said I was walking away. I knew that if I'd gotten this far without them, I could do it again.

The next week I had a call with my executive at AVGP. I decided to lay it all out there and said, "I think it's time to do a show where a woman gets to *say* she is a stand-up comedian, and there is no woman more qualified than me. This is my life and I want to write about it."

I knew he was going to say no. The silence on the other end of the line told me that this, like so many of my ideas, would be a "hard pass."

Then I heard, "We totally agree." And I said, "In theory, or? . . ."

He laughed. "We want to work with you; we are invested in *you*."

I had never heard those words before! I choked out, "You mean *on this* or like, hypothetically in the future? . . ."

No, he meant this; he meant now.

I added, "I want to write it myself." He said, "We totally agree."

I quickly added, "And . . . I want a pony!" Nothing.

But a few months later, I got to write that pilot myself. And someone even bought it.

I had earned the chance to create the show I wanted on *my* terms. I got there by betting on myself and refusing to sell my ideas short.

This past year of my life has been all about betting on myself, even when it comes to this book. I've pitched versions of *Girl Logic* for years. The talk show I got on Freeform in 2017 was the result of four late-night pilots on three different networks over the course of five years. My first theater tour in 2016 was the result of more than seven years of nonstop road-dogging. My hair is slowly starting to get thicker because I started taking vitamins! See, literally nothing other than zits, regret, and flowers bloom overnight.

Figuring out what makes you happy can be a minute-to-minute adventure or a lifelong endeavor, but never stop. I know one thing for sure: whatever you want is out there, and the universe wants you to find it. (Unless it's thinner thighs, in which case I'm pretty sure I'll be taunted by the universe forever.)

Afterword

I Care, You Care, We All Care, but . . . Not All the Time

This book was not written as an autobiography because, at thirty-four, I still don't feel I have accomplished enough to write it all down and say, "This is the story of how I made it." The reality is, I haven't "made it" yet, and, even when I do, I doubt I will realize it. If anything, I could offer a guide on how to work really hard to get to the middle and explain the journey thus far. But I know about how girls think, I know what hard work in stand-up feels like, and I know that I have so much more to learn and accomplish. I also thought that writing from the perspective of someone still in the trenches would be helpful. Hindsight always brings relief. Once you've made your money and become a success, it's easy to spout out platitudes like "just enjoy the ride." But it's hard to enjoy the ride when it's making you nauseous and scared and you aren't sure when it will be over. I wrote this book while on the ride. I'll let you know how I feel when it's over.

As a woman in comedy, I have to lead with strength. As I did the emotional excavating of writing this book, I realized that something born out of necessity has grown into something of a detriment for me: I might be too tough. I know I've preached the idea that a woman can't be too confident, and I definitely still believe that. But, on a personal note, being constantly prepared to fight has become . . . exhausting. I walk around tense and hypervigilant, poised to strike.

It's only within the past year that I've learned to let go of my obsession with what everyone else is doing and what everyone else thinks of me. I finally began to chill and take comfort in the fact that all I can do is, well, what I'm doing. Part of it came because I realized that I was fighting against something that would never change. People would never stop moving past me, things would never completely go my way. . . . But I would never stop trying. Me trying was the only thing I could control. That and not looking at social media as much! It's all poison. It just reminds you that you aren't perfect enough, famous enough, accomplished enough, and that everyone around you is dying of cancer and the planet is turning into a giant ball of melted ice caps and plastic. Want to know why you have anxiety? Because you hit the "Discover" button on Instagram too much.

It can be hard to play passive, sit back, and not care. Or even pretend to not care. Women are taught that a lot of our success rides on our ability to be likeable. Men, however, are lauded for being stoic and remote, for not giving a fuck. On them, that's considered attractive. No one questions what men are giving up by being so strong. No one says, "Sure, he kicks ass in the boardroom but he had to give up having kids." No one calls a man an ice queen when he's standoffish, says he just needs to get laid when he's frustrated, or asks, "Wow, what'd your dad do to you?" when he's angry.

And this? It all just makes me even more determined to be true to myself in every circumstance. It no longer matters to me what people think of my strength, my occasional aloofness, or my bouts of rage about the state of humanity. I'm a woman and I get mad. Don't like it? Look away.

Of course, Girl Logic makes it incredibly difficult to not give a fuck what people think of you, your decisions, your job, your . . . everything. Again, there's the likability factor. Other people's perceptions are a far greater enemy to women than they are to men, and they can be deadly. "She seems slutty," "She seems like a ball buster," "She seems like someone who reminds me of someone who hurt me. . . . " Some days all you can think is, "WHY TRY?!"

The thing is, I have no interest in superfluous pain. I like winning, but I never throw the first punch. I don't have the energy to try to win every fight anymore, and walking around constantly preparing myself to do battle only keeps me in a perpetual state of tension and anxiety. For years, if I looked at the Comedy Store lineup and saw a comic's name that I didn't like, for any reason—competition, disagreements, or even just random awkwardness—I would spend all night feeling nervous about running into them. One day I just stopped. I started asking myself, "What's the worst that could possibly happen?" Are they gonna pull me aside and attack me? Nope. Worst case, we see each other, nod, and keep walking. It's crazy how often we forget to have a rational discussion with ourselves about the worst possible outcome.

See, somewhere between putting too much weight on being liked and being obnoxiously selfish lies your individual version of bliss. Everyone wants to be loved; everyone wants to feel included and appreciated. (Sometimes, the shittier someone is, the more they need outright adulation.) Women should be especially mindful of this as we claw our way to happiness. Give another girl a compliment every now and again, knowing she took just as long to get ready as you did (and her Girl Logic probably erroneously convinced her nothing in her closet would ever look cute enough). Be kind, be gracious, be above it all, and if none of that works, fuck what anyone else thinks— you tried.

It might sound cynical, but one major lesson I've learned by living in Hollywood is that nothing we do *really* matters. That red-carpet dress you spent weeks finding? No one is gonna remember it next year. That date you went on when you gave the guy a weird impression and he ghosted on you immediately after dropping you off? Guess what—he's married now and doesn't think about you, just like you don't remember half the guys you've blown off. Upsetting people, worrying about outfits, fretting over how you looked or sounded in a conversation—none of it matters because if I asked you right now what you wore or did or said last year on this day, you wouldn't remember. Facebook would, but only your mom is looking through those lame digital albums it makes.

Of course it's hard to remember all that stuff in the moment, when you actually need it. Here's an embarrassing anecdote, though, to illustrate. I remember being at the Netflix Emmy party a few years ago, and *Orange Is the New Black* was the belle of the ball. I don't typically drink at events, but this one was different because, well, I was leaving early to meet a boy. On my way out of the party, I saw Adrienne C. Moore, who plays Tova. I had been so in love with her character arc that season, and I was a huge fan of the show for what it did for women—lesbians and women of color in particular.

Anyway, in my buzzed excitement I trotted up to her and blurted out, "Oh my God, I'm such a fan! You were amazing in the episode when you converted to Judaism!" I was ready for us to bond over that scene; we would swiftly become best friends, obviously. Exhausted, not just from having come from the Governor's Ball, but probably from a lifetime of white girls saying whatever they wanted to her, she looked at me and said, "That's not me."

I was talking to the wrong actress. I was talking to Danielle Brooks, the actress who plays Taystee.

God fucking no, I don't think all black people look alike! It was a mortifying mistake, but I was drunk and overly excited and, to be totally fair, not wearing contacts and coming at her from afar. Regardless, in that moment, I wanted to throw a smoke bomb, yell, "THIS NEVER HAPPENED," and disappear. As a rush of hot embarrassment washed over me, I remembered, "Wait . . . she has no idea who *I* am, and this doesn't need to matter." I said, "I sincerely apologize." She told me it was fine, and I turned on my heels and waited for her to walk away.

I felt horrible! But I took an odd comfort in knowing that what I'd said would probably be the last thing on her mind on a night as big as this. I truly hope she doesn't remember it; I hope I didn't taint her wonderful night with the memory of someone unintentionally saying something stupid. But I was never happier to not be famous and recognizable than in that moment.

If anything, that forgiveness is something I chose to pay forward, a year later, when a waiter scurried up to me at the Upfronts and said "you're my favorite stand up comic, I can't believe I'm blanking on your name! Oh! Ilana Glazer!" Not only do I not look like her, she doesn't do stand up. Still, I knew he was a fan of mine and perhaps simply said the more famous girl whose first name started with I." I smiled, knowing it really didn't matter and knowing he meant well.

Truth is? Though very few things actually matter in the long run, Girl Logic can help you suss out what matters to you, personally, the most. Sure, strive to be kind, but you can't always treat others the way you want to be treated because sometimes "others" are so dense, you're pretty sure clubbing them over the head might be the only thing they'll understand.

I have to stop myself once an hour and remind myself that the universe isn't against me. That the woman in front of me in line at CVS didn't wake up and think, "I'm gonna make Iliza's life miserable today." (Honestly? Try as I might, I do believe there is a secret meeting in Los Angeles every morning at five where people gather and get their "Annoyance Assignments" for the day. I bet people are given tasks like, "just get in your car and drive on the freeway, any freeway; do whatever you can do to create more traffic and not contribute to society. Oh, and make sure that when your car breaks down, you never push it off to the shoulder." Or the people at the airport who don't know the rules. You know the ones. It's like, "WE ARE IN A TSA LINE! YES, YOU HAVE TO THROW OUT YOUR FUCKING WATER! YOU HAVE HAD TO THROW IT OUT FOR THE PAST SIXTEEN YEARS, TODAY ISN'T ANY DIFFERENT! THERE IS STILL A WAR ON TERROR!")

But then I remember it doesn't actually matter, that I don't *have to* give a fuck about every little bump in the road. The minor irritations, the major fuck ups- yes they hurt, and it's a minute to minute conscious decision to move past it and focus on the future.

Girl Logic is all about the gray, and figuring out just how much you actually care about the stuff you think you care about. You'll drain yourself of both energy and fucks-to-give if you throw them at every little thing. But the fact that I'm given the chance to create because I pushed for my chance to create, that's what matters most to me.

Your Girl Logic will prepare you for a million scenarios where things can go utterly wrong, and it will help you survive when everything falls apart. Rejection happens, but unless you're dying, there's no reason you can't use your GL to help you create an even better opportunity. Anything good in this world was created by someone who cared enough to fail over and over. That's why I feel sorry for kids who inherit money (and thereby power): they miss out on the thrill of failure and the rush that comes from rebuilding. See, GL will *always* help you rebuild. Whether it's prompting you to try an insane (and awesome) new look after a terrible breakup, launch a new career after a job loss, shape a new life after a divorce, give chances to people who hurt you, or rethink your idea after you pitch a black version of *Harry Potter* called *Black Magic* that no one was into (I still have the outline if anyone wants), it behooves you to listen to your GL—at least, say, 75 percent of the time.

At the beginning of this book, I explained that Girl Logic makes up the thought processes that help you weigh the past, present, and future in every little decision you make. I also said that most of your decisions won't truly matter in the long run. So what can you do? You can give yourself a break when you're tired, you can work hard when it's important, and you can try to remember that you are the one in charge of your own happiness. Also, I know this is hard to wrap one's mind around, but most people are too selfish to ever try to *make you* unhappy. If someone pisses you off, it's usually by mistake. If it's deliberate, try feeling sorry for them because they're jealous and deranged or they're just a bully who had bad parents.

Finally, allow me to leave you with the tips I give aspiring comics, aside from "be funny":

Be kind.

Work hard.

Don't take shit from anyone.

And remain merciful.